THE LIFE AND WORKS OF
CÉZANNE

THE LIFE AND WORKS OF
CÉZANNE

A COMPREHENSIVE STUDY OF THE ARTIST, HIS LIFE AND CONTEXT,
WITH 500 IMAGES, INCLUDING 300 OF HIS GREATEST PAINTINGS

SUSIE HODGE

HERMES
HOUSE

This edition is published by Hermes House,
an imprint of Anness Publishing Ltd,
Hermes House,
88–89 Blackfriars Road,
London SE1 8HA;
tel. 020 7401 2077; fax 020 7633 9499

www.hermeshouse.com www.annesspublishing.com

Anness Publishing has a new picture agency outlet for
images for publishing, promotions or advertising.
Please visit our website www.practicalpictures.com
for more information.

ETHICAL TRADING POLICY:

Because of our ongoing ecological investment
programme, you, as our customer, can have the
pleasure and reassurance of knowing that a tree is
being cultivated on your behalf to naturally replace
the materials used to make the book you are
holding. For further information about this scheme,
go to www.annesspublishing.com/trees

Publisher: Joanna Lorenz
Project Editor: Anne Hildyard
Designer: Sarah Rock
Proofreading Manager: Lindsay Zamponi
Production Controller: Mai-Ling Collyer

© Anness Publishing Ltd 2010

PUBLISHER'S NOTE

Although the advice and information in this book
are believed to be accurate and true at the time of
going to press, neither the authors nor the publisher
can accept any legal responsibility or liability for any
errors or omissions that may have been made.

PICTURE ACKNOWLEDGEMENTS

akg-images: 1, 5tr; The Bridgeman Art Library: 2, 3,5tl.
AKG: Art Focus Gallery, Zürich, Switzerland: 174b;
Bettina Berggruen (on loan from) Nationalgalerie, Berlin,
Germany: 75t; Bridgestone Museum of Art, Tokyo: 128c;
Brooklyn Museum, USA: 73t; Bucharest National Museum
of Art, Romania: 231b; E. G. Bührle Collection, Zürich,
Switzerland: 175b; Carlsberg Glyptotek, Copenhagen,
Denmark: 191b; Cincinnati Art Museum, USA: 29b;
Cleveland Museum of Art, Ohio, USA: 220; Columbus
Museum of Art, Ohio, USA: 154c; Fine Arts Museum,
San Francisco, USA: 237b; Fondation Beyeler, Basel,
Switzerland: 194b, 243t, 244c; Galeria Nazionale d'Arte
Moderna, Rome: 103; Göteborgs Konstmuseum, Sweden:
148b; Graphische Albertina, Vienna, Austria: 179b;
Guggenheim Museum, New York, USA: 100, 241t;
Hermitage, St Petersburg, Russia: 97b, 210t, 248c; The
Israel Museum, Jerusalem, Israel: 197b; Erich Lessing: 75bl;
Jan Krugier and Marie-Anne Krugier-Poniatowski: 170b,
228b; Kunsthaus, Zürich, Switzerland: 33b, 143t, 157b,
159b; Kunsthalle, Bremen, Germany: 232b; Kunstmuseum,
Basel, Switzerland: 117b; Langmatt Foundation, Baden,
Switzerland: 240t; Mattioli Collection, Milan, Italy: 231t;
Metropolitan Museum of Art, New York, USA: 5r, 219t;
Musée de l'Orangerie, Paris, France: 118b, 152b, 156t;
Musée d'Orsay, Paris, France: 108r, 111, 125t, 244b, 247b;
Musée du Louvre, Paris, France: 96; Musée du Petits
Palais, Paris, France: 16l, 16r, 105 (both), 135c, 171t;

Musée Picasso, Paris, France: 143b; Museu de Arte, Sao
Paulo, Brazil: 204; Museum Folkwang, Essen, Germany:
238t; Museum of Fine Arts, Boston, USA: 56l, 235t;
Museum of Fine Arts, Budapest: 67t, 159t; Museum of
Fine Arts, Houston, Texas, USA: 149t, 194t;
Nasjonalgalleriet, Oslo, Norway: 209t, 232t;
Nationalgalerie, Berlin, Germany: 1, 8; National Gallery of
Canada, Ottawa, Canada: 248t; Dr Peter Nathan, Zürich:
33t; National Gallery of Art, Washington, DC, USA:
145b, 198b; National Gallery of Victoria, Melbourne,
Australia: 163b; Nelson Atkins Museum of Art, Kansas
City, USA: 97c, 250b; Norton Gallery and School of Art,
Florida, USA: 238b; Neue Pinakothek, Munich: 114t, 160;
Oeffentliche Kunstsammlung, Basel: 40b; Galerie
Belvedere, Vienna, Austria: 243b; Philadelphia Museum of
Art, USA: 66b, 221t; Phillips Collection, Washington,
USA: 249b; Photograph: 40t, 107t; Private Collection:
37tl, 52, 64l, 66t, 112b, 114b, 116, 117c, 123b, 132b,
135b, 137t, 138b, 140b, 145t, 148t, 153 (both), 157t,
166b, 167t, 170t, 171b, 174t, 179c, 186b, 197t, 201t,
208t, 211b, 212t, 222b, 227t, 235b, 237t, 237c, 239b,
244t, 245 (both), 248b, 249t, 250t, 251b; Pushkin
Museum, Moscow, Russia: 104b, 236; Rhode Island
Museum of Art, Providence, USA: 206b; Karl und Juerg
Im Obersteg: 55t; Villa Flora: 7b, 57b, 189b; Staatliche
Kunsthalle, Karlsruhe: 41t; Staatsgalerie, Stuttgart,
Germany: 84t, 156b; Stedelijk Museum, Amsterdam, The
Netherlands: 208b; Szepmüveszeti Muzeum, Budapest:
56t, 127t; The Toledo Museum of Art, Ohio, USA: 191t,
226b; Thyssen-Bornemisza Museum 251c; Von der Heydt-
Museum, Wuppertal, Germany: 132t, 175t; Wadsworth
Atheneum, Connecticut, USA: 168; Walker Art Gallery,
Liverpool, UK: 110b.
Alamy: 10, 17bl, 20, 23t, 48t, 48bl, 48br, 49, 50t, 50b,
59tl, 59bl, 68, 76 (both), 77b, 82t, 83t, 89tl, 89b, 91b,
99br; Barnes Foundation, PA, USA: 225t; Courtauld
Institute, London, UK: 195t; Hermitage, St Petersburg,
Russia: 110c, 136t; Kunsthalle, Hamburg, Germany: 122b;
Metropolitan Museum of Art, New York, USA: 106b;
Museu de Arte, Sao Paulo, Brazil: 112t; Musée de
l'Orangerie, Paris, France: 154b, 182t; Musée d'Orsay,
Paris, France: 118t, 119t, 140c, 151t; Nationalgalerie,
Berlin, Germany: 113t; National Gallery, London, UK:
234t, 242t; Narodni Galerie, Prague, Czech Republic:
227b; Private Collection:166t, 230t; Pushkin Museum,
Moscow, Russia: 193b, 249c; Städtische Kunsthalle,
Mannheim, Germany: 212c.
Art Archive: Alfredo Dagli Orti: 79b, 92l, 92br, 119b;
Armand Hammer Museum of Art at UCLA, USA: 177b;
Banco Central de Venezuela: 19b; Bibliothèque des Arts
Décoratifs, Paris, France: 12b, 22b; Burrell Collection,
Glasgow, UK: 158b; Gianni Dagli Orti: 15tr; Louvre,
Paris,: 25t; Musée de l'Orangerie, Paris, France: 70b, 177t;
Musée d'Orsay, Paris, France: 23b, 27bl, 31b, 39t, 39b,
42t, 43l, 47b, 69b, 109t, 126t, 131t, 193t, 226t; National
Gallery of Art, Washington DC, USA: 55b; National
Gallery, London, UK: 92tr; Private Collection: 88, 95t;
Pushkin Museum, Moscow, Russia: 59r; Städtische
Kunsthalle, Mannheim, Germany: 93.
Bridgeman: Allen Memorial Art Museum, Oberlin
college, Ohio, USA: 162b; Art Gallery and Museum,
Kelvingrove, Glasgow, UK: 138t, 144b; Art Gallery of
New South Wales, Sydney, Australia: 44r; Ashmolean
Museum, Oxford, UK: 162t; Bibliothèque des Arts
Décoratifs, Paris, France: 13b, 18r; Bibliothèque
Nationale, Paris, France: 15b; Bridgestone Museum of
Art, Tokyo: 202b; Cleveland Museum of Art, Ohio, USA:
200t; Courtauld Institute Galleries, London, UK: 82b,
192b, 218b, 228t; Detroit Institute of Arts, MI, USA: 189t,
242t; Fitzwilliam Museum, University of Cambridge, UK:
5l, 13t; Fogg Art Museum, Harvard, USA: 3, 178; State
Hermitage, St Petersburg, Russia: 94l, 97t, 192t, 212b,

240b; Indianapolis Museum of Art, USA: 184t; Kimbell
Art Museum, TX, USA: 214b; Kunsthalle, Basel,
Switzerland: 199; Kunsthaus, Zürich, Switzerland: 28t, 58,
61tl; Kunstmuseum, Basel, Switzerland: 109b, 125c;
Metropolitan Museum of Art, New York, USA: 30l, 130b,
191c; Minneapolis Institute of Arts, MN, USA: 80; Musée
Carnavalet, Paris, France: 18l, 21br, 81t, 81bl; Musée de
l'Orangerie, Paris, France: 61b, 222t; Musée du Louvre,
Paris, France: 21tr, 22t, 34r, 144t; Musée du Petit-Palais,
Paris, France: 87tl, 90l, 234b; Musée d'Orsay, Paris,
France: 32b, 34l, 44l, 45t, 46l, 47t, 75bl, 87b, 94r, 106t,
110t, 124, 179t, 214t; Musée Granet, Aix-en-Provence,
France: 32t, 104t; Museu Calouste Gulbenkian, Lisbon,
Portugal: 211; Museum of Finnish Art, Helsinki, Finland:
69tl; Nationalgalerie, Berlin, Germany: 62; National
Gallery, London, UK: 188b; National Gallery of Art,
Washington DC, USA: 31t; National Museum, Stockholm,
Sweden: 91t, 146, 161c; National Museum of Wales, UK:
6t, 67b, 182t, 250c; Neue Pinakothek, Munich: 172b;
Portland Art Museum, OR, USA: 117t; Private Collection:
2, 6b, 17br, 25bl, 29t, 46r, 81br, 86, 95b, 99bl, 102, 107b,
108l, 127b, 130t, 134, 135t, 136b, 137b, 141, 142b, 150
(both), 152t, 154t, 155, 172c, 176t, 186t, 198c, 206t, 218b,
224b, 247t; Pushkin Museum, Moscow, Russia: 36, 41b,
172t, 180t, 196t; Sheffield Galleries and Museum Trust, UK:
128t; Solomon R Guggenheim Museum, New York, USA:
54b; Tokyo Fuji Art Museum, Tokyo, Japan: 122t; Van der
Heydt Museum, Wuppertal, Germany; 165.
Corbis: Albright-Knox Art Gallery, New York, USA: 147t,
246b; Alfredo Dagli Orti: 63tr, 71t, 84b; Art Institute of
Chicago, IL, USA: 205b; Baltimore Museum of Art, MD,
USA: 233t; Barnes Foundation, PA, USA: 139b, 149b,
181t, 207b, 217t, 223, 225b, 229, 233b, 241b, 246t;
Bettmann, Paris, France: 14; Bridgestone Museum of Art,
Tokyo: 200b; Buhrle Collection, Zürich, Switzerland:
201b; Burstein Collection: 65r; Chris Hellier: 79tr;
Christie's: 38, 72r, 85t; Corbis Art: 65l, 74, 90r; Corbis
Museum: 7t, 11, 35r, 42b, 63tl, 63b, 70t, 77t, 79tl, 85b;
115 (both), 128b, 133t; Doug Pearson: 12t; Edsel and
Eleanor Ford House, MI, USA: 221c; Fogg Art Museum,
USA: 184c; Fratelli Alinari: 39l; The Gallery Collection: 26,
27tl; Guggenheim Museum, New York, USA: 247c;
Hermitage, St Petersburg, Russia: 151b; Historical Picture
Library: 24; 27r; 30r; 35t; 37tr; Metropolitan Museum of
Art, New York, USA: 167c, 203b, 205c; Musée d'Orsay,
Paris, France: 139t, 188t, 205t, 224t; Musée Picasso, Paris,
France: 142t; Museum of Fine Arts, USA: 202t; Museum
Folkwang, Essen, Germany: 196b; National Gallery of Art,
Washington DC, USA: 133b; Philadelphia Museum of
Art, USA: 69t, 72l, 147c, 147b, 161b, 169 (all), 180b,
183b, 184b, 187b, 190, 217b; Private Collection: 140t,
164, 187b, 203t, 213, 221b; Pushkin Museum, Moscow,
Russia: 198t; Value Art: 53, 54t, 56r, 60, 71b, 73b, 113b,
120, 123t, 131b; Rijksmuseum Kröller-Müller, The
Netherlands: 183t; Worcester Art Museum, MA, USA:
207t; Yokohama Museum of Art, Japan: 216b.
Getty: AFP/Getty Images: 83b; Buhrle Collection, Zürich,
Switzerland: 61tr; Hulton Archive: 19t, 25br, 28b, 37b,
51t, 64r; Musée Bonnat, Bayonne, France: 45b; Musée
Marmottan, Paris, France: 17t; National Gallery, London,
UK: 158t, 176b; New Carlsberg Glyptotek, Copenhagen,
Denmark: 181b; Phillips Collection, Washington DC,
USA: 78; Private Collection: 15tl, 173b.
Photolibrary: Private Collection: 121, 126b, 129, 163t.
Photos12: Art Institute of Chicago, Illinois, IL, USA: 125b;
Musée de l'Orangerie, Paris, France: 211t; Musée du
Louvre, Paris, France: 216t.
Superstock: Bakwin Collection, New York, USA: 98;
Barnes Foundation: 43r; 51b, 89tr, 99t, 173t, 185, 195b,
210b, 215 (both), 219b, 230b, 239t; E.G. Bührle
Collection, Zürich, Switzerland: 251t; Musée de
l'Orangerie, Paris, France: 161t; Private Collection: 209b.

CONTENTS

INTRODUCTION

In his own time, Paul Cézanne was not widely appreciated and was plagued with self-doubt, but he is now perceived as a pioneer in the art of the late 19th and early 20th centuries, influencing many of the future major figures of the art world.

In July 1907, when Pablo Picasso (1881–1973) revealed *Les Demoiselles d'Avignon* to friends and acquaintances in his Parisian studio, he revolutionized the art world. In the foreground of the huge canvas is a still life that he painted in homage to Cézanne, whose work he had seen at the gallery of the art dealer Ambroise Vollard.

CÉZANNE'S INFLUENCE

Les Demoiselles d'Avignon is generally accepted as a major step towards Cubism, and Picasso cited Cézanne as his main inspiration for it. Cubism was a new way of representing reality in art, influenced by Cézanne's later work. Besides Cubism, Cézanne's vision was the starting point for many other 20th-century art movements. His ideas had a profound effect on artists such as Gauguin, Picasso, Malevich, Matisse, Klee, Braque, Gris, Kandinsky and Duchamp. Both Picasso and Matisse – giants of 20th-century art – called Cézanne 'the father of us all.'

FROM MAN TO MASTER

While Cézanne is now considered to be a major pioneer in the development of modern art, this was not the case in 1885, when his best friend Émile Zola (1840–1902) wrote his novel *The Masterpiece*. Zola based his doomed hero on Cézanne, giving him the same physical appearance, stubborn and volatile temperament, shyness with women, ambition and self-doubt, with a growing isolation and reputation for being mad. From Zola's letters, it is clear that he believed Cézanne to be a genius, but his tale of a failed artist ended their long friendship. This dichotomy of genius and failure coloured Cézanne's reputation for at least half a century after his death.

Cézanne's personality cannot be separated from his art. Full of contradictions, he possessed great

Top: Still Life with a Teapot, c.1902–6. *In his later still lifes, Cézanne increasingly treated objects as motifs in a landscape. Thus, the folds of the carpet seem like mountains surrounding the fruit and teapot.*

Above: Apples and Biscuits, c.1877. *Applying the same scrutiny to his still lifes as he did to all of his work, Cézanne's apples are light and bright colours, yet still give the impression of weight and solidity.*

self-belief, but he was also frequently overwhelmed with self-doubt. Cézanne was passionate about painting, but was essentially self-taught. While he took meticulous care with every work, he

was often thrown into despair when he had finished a painting, and felt inadequate because he had yet again failed to realize his ideas. Yet he managed to surmount opposition from

Above: River Bend, c.1865. Once he had been to Paris, Cézanne thickly applied the bold colours he had seen in the work of Delacroix, including Veronese green, yellow ochre and Prussian blue.

his family, his friends and the official art world, working relentlessly to achieve his desired objective of a 'harmony parallel to nature'.

TRUTH TO NATURE

Like his friends the Impressionists, Cézanne was concerned with painting the truth. He once said of Monet, "Monet is only an eye, but my God, what an eye!" However, although he admired Monet and the other Impressionists, he developed ideas beyond painting just what was in front of him, as they did. He wanted to capture the whole of nature, not just a moment when the sun shines on it. While the Impressionists were painting the shimmering light on the streets of Paris and in the surrounding

Right: Plain in Provence, 1886. Using his oil paint as sparingly as he used watercolour, this painting captures the heaviness of a hot summer day across the countryside Cézanne loved.

countryside, Cézanne retreated to Aix-en-Provence to work out a new way of painting. His idea was that beneath every surface there is a solid structure, the foundations upon which nature is built. This structure never changes, no matter what light falls on it. But unlike surface details, the underlying framework is not always apparent, so he had to compose his paintings very carefully. He said that he wanted to "treat nature by the cylinder, the sphere, the cone", meaning that he was looking for simple shapes and structure in everything he depicted. Almost mathematically, he worked out exactly where everything should be on the canvas. Every colour had to be balanced by another; every brushstroke had to be made in the right direction.

REJECTING RULES

Cézanne was the first artist to break completely with traditions of Western painting that dated back to the 15th century, to shift the emphasis of his work toward factors other than realism. It was a radical stance, and the painters of his generation were aware of his genius long before the public and critics. A letter from Pissarro to his son in 1895 says it all: "You wouldn't believe how much trouble I have convincing certain art lovers, friends of the Impressionists, of all the great and rare qualities in Cézanne. I think centuries will pass before people realize this."

CÉZANNE: HIS LIFE AND TIMES

One of the distinctive aspects of Cézanne's art is its apparent objectivity. But for the most part, he was actually interpreting his inner feelings and perceptions of life around him. Looking at his work, his temperament and the struggles and suffering he endured are not obvious, except perhaps in his early dark and violent paintings. As he developed as an artist, his beliefs in nature's connections and interaction increased and he strove to show that everything was interrelated, part of an all-embracing spiritual phenomenon. He spent his life attempting to paint the truth and complexities of nature and ended up as one of the most important artists of the early 20th century.

Left: Still Life with Flowers and Fruit, *1888–90.*

THE REBEL

Cézanne was born toward the middle of the 19th century in southern France. He did not show any early interest in art, but once he had decided on his path, remained focused and resolute. During his lifetime, new artistic methods emerged from rapidly-changing developments in society, technology and culture. Correspondingly, his own approach emerged from a search for a more expressive style that also encompassed his emotions, energy and imagination. Despite enduring ridicule and receiving little recognition, he continued working, and it was only toward the end of his life that he received wide acclaim.

Above: The Four Bathers, c.1876–8.
Left: Still Life with Pot, Bottle, Cup and Fruit, c.1869–71.

AIX-EN-PROVENCE

On 19 January 1839, a bitterly cold day, Paul Cézanne was born in a house in the rue de l'Opéra, a peaceful street in Aix-en-Provence in the south of France. His schooling and the friendships he forged were to directly affect his future.

Cézanne was the eldest child of 40-year-old Louis-Auguste Cézanne and 24-year-old Anne-Elisabeth-Honorine Auburt. His parents did not marry until Cézanne was five years old.

FAMILY CONNECTIONS

Unusually for the time, Louis-Auguste acknowledged his illegitimate son, and the infant was baptized at the church of Sainte-Marie-Madeleine a month after his birth. Soon after the baptism, the family moved to 55 cours Mirabeau, where Louis-Auguste's hat-making business was situated. A second child, Marie, was born two years later, and Cézanne became particularly close to her. Ten years later, another daughter, Rose, was born, but Cézanne never felt any real attachment to his second sister.

THE SUCCESSFUL BUSINESSMAN

In the 19th century, Aix-en-Provence was a picturesque but somewhat isolated city; the railway did not reach it until later in the century. Its main industries were textiles and dyeing works, distilleries and food producers. Just outside the town were the Tholonet quarries, the Célony plasterworks and brickworks. Cézanne's father was a

Above: The countryside of Provence, France. Cézanne was born in Provence in south-eastern France, an area that has hot summers and mild winters.

Below: A schoolroom in mid-19th-century France. Cézanne had a classical education and was more interested in history, mathematics, poetry and literature than art.

ÉMILE ZOLA

The boy who was to become one of the period's most celebrated and controversial literary figures, Émile Zola (1840–1902), was born in Paris but moved to Aix-en-Provence when his father's engineering work took him to the south of France. When Zola was seven, his father died, and his mother was unable to reclaim the money owed for construction work he had already undertaken. They were almost destitute. Then the former French Prime Minister Adolphe Thiers (1797–1877) obtained a bursary for Zola and he attended the Collège Bourbon as a part-boarder. School bullies found the small, lisping, myopic boy easy to pick on. Cézanne, who was physically bigger and in a higher class, stood up for him against the bullies and eventually they left young Zola alone.

shrewd businessman and, with two partners, had established a successful millinery business. Soon he was running the company of Martin, Coupin et Cézanne on his own, and he made a considerable fortune. When Aix-en-Provence's Bank Bargès collapsed in 1848, Louis-Auguste, confident of his business acumen, joined with the bank's head teller, Cabassol, and established the Banque Cézanne et Cabassol. His success continued, and by 1859, he had bought an 18th-century estate, the Jas de Bouffan, which had once been the home of the Governor of Provence.

CÉZANNE'S CHILDHOOD

Despite his financial success, Louis-Auguste was never accepted socially in the town. This was partly because he had not married Anne-Elisabeth before their first two children were born, and partly because he had made his living from millinery and money-lending. He became a virtual recluse, surrounded only by his family. A strict and authoritarian figure, he found it difficult to express his emotions and passed this on to his children. Marie, his favourite, was bold in his company, and her quiet elder brother often hid behind her in their father's presence. He grew up closer to his intelligent, warm-hearted and lively mother, who encouraged and supported him throughout his life.

When he was ten years old, Cézanne was sent to the Jesuit École de Saint-Joseph as a day pupil. He remained there for two years and then went into the first form of the Collège Bourbon at Aix as a boarder in 1852. Children from families in the upper ranks of society attended the Collège Bourbon, and his six years there were similar to the school life of many middle-class boys of his era, including being bullied in the early days. His education was classical and he worked well at the natural sciences, Greek and Latin, and developed a love of the classics and literature in general. More importantly, at the Collège Bourbon he made friends with a skinny boy who was a year younger than him and who was to have a decisive influence on his choice of career.

Above: The Church of Sainte Jean-de-Malte, Aix-en-Provence, *Antoine Fortuné Marion, c.1866–70. Marion (1846–1900) was an amateur painter and one of Cézanne's close friends from Aix.*

Below: Tea in High Society in France, *c.1840, after Achille Deveria. Cézanne's father wanted to be accepted by the bourgeoisie, but Cézanne never felt comfortable in fashionable society.*

THE INSEPARABLES

From the time that Cézanne became Zola's protector and stopped his tormentors from bullying him at school, the two boys became firm friends – a friendship that was to last for many years.

Cézanne was more diligent in his school work than his friend, but Zola was quick-witted, sharp and outspoken. Another boy joined them: Baptistin Baille (1841–1918), who later became a professor of optics and acoustics. The three earned the nickname 'Les Trois Inséparables' (The Three Inseparables) because they were always together.

ACADEMIC PRIZES

No one at school bothered Zola now that he had a protector, although the sons of the local gentry, rich merchants and farmers still sneered at the two boys, calling them Don Quixote and Sancho Panza. Zola copied Cézanne's diligence and he soon won prizes for academic work. Although Cézanne earned prizes for his school work too, especially in mathematics, Greek and history, he was not noted for his artistic skills (although he once received a runner-up award for drawing). Ironically, it was Zola, not Cézanne, who won several school drawing prizes.

The friends spent all their free time together, rambling in the local countryside and fishing and swimming in the River Arc. They discussed art and literature, in particular the Romantics, and they read Homer and Virgil together. The boys also wrote verse in Latin. Zola commented: "You have a writer in you, just as I have. My verses are probably purer than yours, but yours are definitely more poetic and true. You write with your heart, I write with my head."

COUNTRY RAMBLES

The boys sometimes walked as far as the Bibémus quarry, the Château de Galice, the slopes of Les Lauves or the Gorges d'Infernets, where Zola's father, the engineer, had built a dam. From

Below: The Congress of Paris in 1856. After almost three years of the Crimean War, the Congress of Paris was called, in an attempt to create peace between the warring nations.

these vantage points, they could see views of the town and surrounding area that became focal points of Cézanne's later paintings. Their favourite walk was to the village of Tholonet and it must have been at this time that Cézanne developed his passion for such landscapes. In 1856, he began attending evening classes to learn drawing at the Aix-en-Provence Art School.

It was one of the few periods of his life in which he felt completely happy. In later years, Zola wrote of it, "There were three of us friends, three mischievous kids who were still grinding away at school work. On holidays and times when we could get away from study, we would go charging off at top speed into the country. We needed fresh air, sunshine… In the winter we adored the cold and the crisp, echoing crunch of the frozen ground beneath our feet." Meanwhile, Cézanne's difficult personality was emerging. He often flew into unpredictable rages, usually stemming from lack of self-confidence.

THE JOLLY FELLOWS

Cézanne and Zola also amused themselves by playing and composing music. Zola started a band called The Jolly Fellows. He played the clarinet and Cézanne the cornet. Although Zola later lost his enthusiasm for music, Cézanne retained a passion for it throughout his whole life.

SEPARATION OF THE INSEPARABLES

The Three Inseparables were abruptly separated in February 1858 when Zola and his mother moved to Paris. Zola had failed his *baccalauréat* exam and his mother's hopes for a law career for him were dashed. Court cases over money owed to her had drained what finances

Above: December in Provence, *Henry Herbert La Thangue (1859–1929), c.1890. Many other artists recognized the serene allure of the landscape and the golden light in Provence.*

she had, and she hoped that life in Paris would be cheaper and that her son might find some employment there.

Above: The countryside of Provence. The wild areas of Provence were perfect places for Cézanne, Zola and Baille to explore during any season, and may have provided inspiration for Cézanne.

He began working as a clerk in a shipping firm. Zola wrote to Cézanne frequently, recalling their time in Aix-en-Provence fondly and trying to persuade his friend to follow him to Paris and begin his career as an artist. Knowing Cézanne's character well, he described how he could make progress without wasting time, which he knew would be one of his main concerns: "From six to eleven in the morning you could do life painting in a studio school, then you could have your lunch and from twelve to four in the afternoon you could copy a masterpiece which particularly appealed to you in the Louvre or the Luxembourg Museum."

Left: Émile Zola with his family. Cézanne's friendship with Zola started when they were boys and spanned 40 years. They had many interests in common and still managed to maintain a lively correspondence in later life.

SOCIAL STATUS

Cézanne's father was a self-taught, self-made man who, through diligence and determination, had made a lot of money, but had not attained social standing. He thus wanted his son to establish a career in law or banking to achieve a good position in society.

With the aim of making his snobbish neighbours reconsider his business achievements, Louis-Auguste wanted his eldest child to forge a career in law or banking, and so achieve a good position in society.

LAW LECTURES AND ART CLASSES

Money meant everything to Louis-Auguste, and in his mind, any career other than banking or law was out of the question for his son. So after obtaining his *baccalauréat*, rather than following Zola to Paris, Cézanne complied with his father's wishes and enrolled at the Faculty of Law at the University of Aix-en-Provence. In his spare time, he continued writing poetry, drawing, fishing, swimming and climbing Mont Sainte-Victoire. He wrote to Zola complaining that he did not find law appealing. The course was dull and his prospects were even duller – he was supposed to be joining his father's bank after his finals. Meanwhile, he was still continuing his classes at the local art school, the Municipal School of Drawing, fitting them around his law course. There he met several old school friends and enjoyed the traditional teaching by Joseph Gibert. Gibert was a methodical, conventional painter and the established methods he taught Cézanne were extremely useful to him later on. Gibert held early-morning life classes on Mondays, Tuesdays and Fridays, from six till eight in the summer and from seven till nine in the winter. He also taught his students to draw, to paint in oils and watercolours and to make copies of the paintings, lithographs and sculptures in the Musée Granet.

THE JAS DE BOUFFAN

In 1859, Louis-Auguste Cézanne bought the dilapidated house that had once belonged to the Governor of Provence, the Jas de Bouffan. This imposing 18th-

century manor house and farm with its mature tree-lined drive needed extensive renovations. Louis-Auguste allowed his son to create four large panels to decorate the salon. For his first large works, he painted colourful allegories of the four seasons. The style is rather stiff, the images classically inspired. Later, he painted a portrait of

Above: Summer, *Above left:* Winter, 1860–2. These are Cézanne's first known paintings. As a joke, he signed each one 'Ingres', as this was the artist academic painters modelled themselves on.

his father reading a newspaper, which was added to the room's decorations. The Jas de Bouffan came to mean a

THE MUSÉE GRANET

The Municipal School of Drawing was accommodated in this local gallery. Works of art there included paintings by lesser-known French and Italian masters, including the work of François-Marius Granet (1775–1849), who had been a friend of Ingres. Cézanne admired all the works, but particularly the classical paintings, and watercolours of Mont Sainte-Victoire executed in the style of the English landscape painters. One of the paintings he copied there was cherished by his mother and she kept it with her for the rest of her life.

great deal to Cézanne throughout his life. He later set up a studio at the top of the house, but he was happiest working in the tranquil grounds of the property.

YEARNING FOR PARIS

One of the benefits of Louis-Auguste's wealth was that he followed the common practice of paying another man to do his son's compulsory military service. But instead of applying himself to the law in gratitude, Cézanne began neglecting his legal studies, becoming increasingly listless and obsessed with going to Paris to study art. His father's response was, "Genius keeps no man

alive, but money does". It was a difficult time for Louis-Auguste. His 20-year-old son, who had been given an extremely comfortable middle-class upbringing and education, was untidy, inarticulate, withdrawn and somewhat ill-mannered. He stopped turning up for his law lectures and pleaded with his mother to help him to persuade his father to allow him to study art in Paris. The lure of

Below: The Jas de Bouffan. The mature chestnut tree-lined avenue leading up to the family's large country house, the Jas de Bouffan, features in many of Cézanne's paintings.

Above: The Studio of Baron Antoine Jean Gros, Auguste Antoine Masse (1795–1836), c.1830. This is a typical, traditional 19th-century life class in France. Only male students were allowed to draw the nude.

galleries, official annual Salon exhibitions and top-quality tuition preoccupied him, and confrontations with his father occurred frequently. Eventually, his father relented and in April 1861, Louis-Auguste and Cézanne's sister Marie accompanied him to Paris, where they made sure he was happily settled, and left him with a small allowance.

Above: Mont Sainte-Victoire seen from Cézanne's road. This view greeted Cézanne each day from his home at the Jas de Bouffan. It was a subject that he painted over and over again in later life.

CÉZANNE IN PARIS

The 1860s were an exciting time to be in Paris and Cézanne arrived there full of optimism, believing that at last he could make something of his ambition to become an artist. He met Pissarro, an Impressionist, who was to become a friend as well as a mentor.

The art world of Paris was changing, although it was not a smooth transition. New ideas about style and the approach to art were emerging rapidly as technology and society developed, but were being equally rapidly suppressed by the official art academies.

THE OLD GUARD

Jean-Auguste-Dominique Ingres (1780–1867) and also Eugène Delacroix (1798–1863) had long been held as the model exponents of great art. Ingres was acknowledged for his neo-classical lines and impeccable draughtsmanship, while Delacroix epitomized the fluid, colourful, dynamic approach of the Romanticists. Although Cézanne and Zola had talked about Romantic art and literature during their walks in Aix, Cézanne had not encountered Delacroix's work until this first visit to Paris. At the time, Delacroix was completing two large, dynamic murals in the church of Saint Sulpice: *The Expulsion of Heliodorus* and *Jacob Wrestling with the Angel.*

NEW ART

Yet, while Ingres and Delacroix painted idealized stories, Gustave Courbet (1819–77) had recently been producing and exhibiting quite the opposite: paintings that depicted the ordinary world around him. Not only did that defy accepted conventions in painting,

Above: New façade of the Louvre, 1861. By the time Cézanne arrived in 1861, most of the modernization of Paris was complete. This was the impressive new façade of the Musée du Louvre.

Left: The Moulin de la Galette, Montmartre, Antoine Vollon (1833–1900), 1861. The Moulin de la Galette, a windmill at the top of the hill at Montmartre, was turned into a fashionable nightclub, known for its relaxed and welcoming atmosphere.

but also his painting technique, with its strong tonal contrasts applied quickly with a palette knife, resulting in a coarsely textured surface, was considered objectionable. In 1855, when his work had been rejected by the Exposition Universelle, he had set up his own pavilion and displayed about 40 of his paintings there.

By 1861, when Cézanne arrived in Paris, Courbet had gained considerable prestige among avant-garde artists, although the official art world still regarded him as a maverick. His technique derived from 17th-century Spanish masters whose paintings hung in the Louvre, including Diego Velázquez (1599–1660), Francisco Zurbarán (1598–1664) and Jusepe de Ribera (1591–1652). When Cézanne saw his works for the first time, he became strongly influenced by Courbet's innovative style.

Above: The Pont Neuf, 1865. A photograph of the Pont Neuf by the Île de la Cité in 1865. The fashionably attired promenading Parisians made Cézanne feel homesick for the simplicity of Aix.

ACADÉMIE SUISSE

With his father's allowance of 125 francs a month, Cézanne rented furnished rooms on the rue des Feuillantines, not far from his friend Zola's accommodation in the Panthéon quarter. Cézanne enrolled at the Académie Suisse, a private atelier run by Charles Suisse, a former model of the painter Jacques-Louis David (1748–1825). It was not a conventional school, but a freely run space where art students sat in a rather grubby room on the second floor of an old building near the Pont Saint-Michel. They paid ten francs each a month to work from a life model rather than from plaster

casts, which was the established method for students. With no restrictions, corrections or examinations, they were allowed to work in their own style and to use their own choice of materials. Even the class timings were flexible, so that students could decide when to attend. For Cézanne, the attraction was the Académie's former pupils. Some years before, Richard Parkes Bonington (1802–28), Delacroix and Courbet had met there. By the time Cézanne enrolled, Camille Pissarro (1830–1903) had been going there since 1855, Claude Monet (1840–1926) had joined in 1859, although he was conscripted to Algeria within a couple of months of Cézanne's arrival, and Armand Guillaumin (1841–1927) enrolled at the same time as Cézanne. The forward-thinking atmosphere appealed to Cézanne. He and Pissarro established a friendship from the start. Another artist at the Académie was a man Cézanne had met at the Municipal Drawing School in Aix: Achille Emperaire (1828–98). Cézanne had always admired Emperaire's work, and because he was a dwarf and hunchback, Cézanne saw him as a fellow outsider, misunderstood by the world.

Below: The Artist's Studio, Caracas, Camille Pissarro, 1854. Eight years before they met, Pissarro had spent a year in Caracas, Venezuela. Although he was nine years older than Cézanne, the two became close friends.

THE MODERNIZATION OF PARIS

The whole layout of Paris was being radically changed between 1852 and 1870. Baron Haussmann, the prefect of the Seine département, oversaw the design and rebuilding, turning Paris from a medieval town into a modern city, with straight, wide boulevards replacing the cramped and irregular streets, and cafés, shops, parks, museums and an opera house that was created in the neo-classical style.

THE MUSÉE DU LOUVRE

Cézanne's arrival in Paris coincided with the popular annual art exhibition known
as the Salon, where new paintings were exhibited in the Musée du Louvre. He visited
the exhibition with Zola and was enthralled.

Cézanne marvelled at the great skill and interesting ideas of some of the artists showing paintings in the Salon, and scoffed at others. He deplored any showiness, and to him, many of the works were just ostentatious displays of technical skill, with little substance. Although artists such as Courbet had already caused scandal by not painting in the established, expected way, there was still a battle to be fought before artists could paint however they wanted without recriminations.

COPYING THE GREAT MASTERS

As soon as he reached Paris, Cézanne visited the Louvre, the Luxembourg Palace and the royal château at Versailles. These were places where he could learn from the great artists. He became a regular visitor to the Louvre, where he studied the collections and copied works by Titian (c.1490–1576), Rubens (1577–1640), Michelangelo (1475–1564), Giorgione (c.1478–1510), Velázquez, Raphael (1483–1520), Zurbarán and Ribera. He was not aiming for technical accuracy as most

art students were, but rather took various ideas and characteristics from the works he admired, including paint application methods, compositional styles, choice of palette and unusual handling of subjects. He built up a routine, attending the Académie Suisse in the mornings and copying in the Louvre in the afternoons. He particularly admired Rubens, the Spanish masters and Delacroix.

CÉZANNE THE MISFIT

But Paris was not as he had expected it to be. The chaos caused by the modernization and rebuilding was difficult to live with, and his own boarding house was frequented by prostitutes and thieves and was often raided by the police. He also found that the new boulevards, cafés and clubs

that were already established attracted fashionable men and women dressed in their finery at all hours of the day and night. Cézanne felt that he did not fit in. He was acutely aware of his southern accent and awkward manner, and the other artists at the Académie Suisse often teased him. His furious reactions earned him the nickname 'L'écorché' (the man without skin), implying that he was hypersensitive. Although Pissarro took his part against the others, Cézanne became depressed and began to talk about going back to Aix. Zola wrote to their friend Baille:

Below: The Death of St Bonaventura,
*Zurbarán, 1629. Zurbarán's dramatic
scenes of social realism in rich colours and
his strong contrasts of tone influenced
Cézanne greatly.*

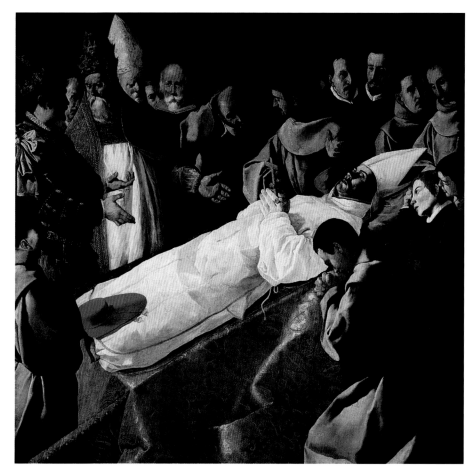

THE SALON

The Paris Salon was the annual art exhibition of the École des Beaux-Arts (the official art school). First introduced in the 17th century, it was held in the Louvre until the end of the 19th century, and by the time Cézanne arrived in Paris, it had become the most important art exhibition in the world. Originally established to exhibit the work of final-year students, it was soon extended to any artist who wanted to submit work for the selection committee. If their work was exhibited, artists' reputations were usually established.

Right: The Holy Family, *Raphael, 1518. Cézanne revered Raphael, and this painting's complex composition, muted tones and elegant drapery fascinated him.*

"To prove he has lost none of his eccentricity, I need only tell you that the moment he arrived here he was talking of returning to Aix. He fought for three years to come here and now he doesn't give a fig for it all." In an effort to prevent him leaving Paris, Zola asked him to paint his portrait. Twice Cézanne began the portrait, but each time he gave up in despair.

ESCAPE TO AIX

One day Zola arrived for a sitting, to find his friend with his bags packed and the portraits destroyed. Cézanne returned to Aix in the autumn of 1861. Frustrated with his friend's lack of tenacity in making a go of life in Paris, Zola wrote to Baille: "To prove something to Cézanne would be like trying to persuade the towers of Notre Dame to dance a quadrille... nothing can bend him."

Above: Boy with Cherries, *Édouard Manet (1832–83), 1859. The artists at the Académie Suisse, where Cézanne studied, often discussed Manet's independent style and fresh ideas.*

Right: The Finished Louvre, *French School, c.1861. On his arrival in Paris, Cézanne visited the Louvre often, studying and copying from his favourite artists.*

PROVENCE TO PARIS

Back in Aix, disillusioned and despondent, Cézanne succumbed to paternal pressure and began working as a clerk in the Banque Cézanne et Cabassol. However, he spent a few months painting around the Jas de Bouffan before returning to Paris.

THE CAFÉ GUERBOIS

During the 19th century in Paris, working men frequented cafés for midday meals or to relax with friends in the evenings. The Café Guerbois in the Batignolles quarter was just such a venue. It had become a popular meeting place for artists and writers, who were often known as the Batignolles group. Manet, Zola, Pissarro, Monet, Frédéric Bazille (1841–70), Edgar Degas (1834–1917), Auguste Renoir (1841–1919) and Alfred Sisley (1839–99) were a few of the artists who gathered there, often conducting lively and heated debates.

Cézanne rejoined the Municipal School of Drawing in Aix, attending classes in the evenings, and spent any spare time he had painting in the tranquil surroundings of the farm and meadows of his family home.

Above: Landscape with a Castle, *Rembrandt van Rijn (1606–69), c.1632. Cézanne was captivated by Rembrandt's handling of paint, dramatic compositions and creation of atmosphere.*

Below: Café des Ambassadeurs, *Champs-Élysées, Paris, c.1840. The Café des Ambassadeurs was a restaurant and nightclub that was popular with the French bourgeoisie, although not with Cézanne.*

THE JAS DE BOUFFAN

Cézanne's personality was full of contradictions. He craved recognition but was fairly shy; he was ambitious but filled with doubts; he was timid but cantankerous, proud but sensitive, obstinate but changeable, and perhaps most of all, independent, often at odds with his father, but unusually attached to his family home at the Jas de Bouffan. The rather grand manor house with its vast grounds was, throughout his life, the place where he felt happiest and most relaxed. For the months after his return from Paris, he spent much of his time there, sketching and painting. He also made numerous studies of male nudes which followed the academic style of life drawing.

Right: Outskirts of a Village near Beauvais, *Corot, c.1850. Corot was one of the first artists who painted complete canvases en plein air, a practice that was considered unrefined by the École des Beaux-Arts.*

THE LURE OF PARIS

After a few months, however, he wondered if he had been a little impetuous in leaving Paris so hastily. He felt restless and unsuited to his post at the bank, and he missed seeing the exciting developments and changes in art. He decided that if he went to Paris but returned to Provence frequently, he would overcome the dreadful homesickness he felt when he was away from home for too long. He wrote to Zola about the idea and in September 1862, Zola replied: "I approve completely of your idea of coming to Paris to work and then retiring to Provence." So he once again confronted his father, who had almost become accustomed to the inevitability of his son not following him into the family bank. Although he was hugely disappointed, Louis-Auguste accepted his son's resolve and allowed him to leave the bank and return to Paris. He made some stipulations, however, which

Below: At the Bourse, *Edgar Degas, c.1879. Haussmann's regeneration of Paris boosted the French economy. This painting by Cézanne's contemporary Degas exemplifies the confidence of the Paris Stock Exchange.*

included enrolling at the official art school, the École des Beaux-Arts, and dedicating himself completely to his academic art studies.

RETURN TO PARIS

In November 1862, at the age of 23, Cézanne returned to Paris with his monthly 125-franc allowance from his father. He found rooms in a quiet street near the Jardin du Luxembourg and applied to the École des Beaux-Arts as instructed by his father, but he failed the entrance exam. The report on his work stated: "Cézanne has the temperament of a colourist but he exaggerates." He was not upset; he had expected this reaction as he did not conform to the academic style of painting, with its perfect draughtsmanship, invisible brush marks, smooth paint and precedence of historical subjects over landscape. He re-enrolled at the Académie Suisse, where he had always wanted to be. He was delighted to get back to discussing the new ideas of Realism with reference to Courbet and Jean-Baptiste-Camille Corot's (1796–1875) paintings, while Édouard Manet was initiating intense discussions about the purpose and direction of art. Cézanne concurred with the annoyance these avant-garde thinkers felt about the inflexible attitudes of official art circles. As soon as he resumed classes at the Académie Suisse, he made more of an effort to get along with the other students and to socialize with them at the Café Guerbois.

THE SALON

Cézanne was determined to make more progress in Paris this time. He began forming his own independent ideas about colour and structure, and his ambition to be recognized and accepted in the art world became more resolute.

Spurred on by Zola's support, dedication and application, Cézanne began preparing to submit work to the Salon. If he could attain official recognition in that way, then his difficult relationship with his father would be ameliorated; what is more, he would gain respect and earn his own living.

WORKING IN PARIS

In November 1862, once Cézanne had settled down in Paris, he led a simple and studious life. He was able to live almost comfortably thanks to his father's allowance (and possibly some assistance from his mother). He often copied paintings by Delacroix, such as those on show at the Musée du Luxembourg and in the chapel of the Saints-Anges at Saint Sulpice. He felt happier than he had during his previous stay in Paris and although he did not visit the cafés as often as his fellow artists, when he did, he tried not to be rude.

AMBITION AND COMPROMISE

Every year, hopeful artists submitted works to the government-sponsored Salon jury. The selection committee was made up mainly of artists who worked in the academic style and their outlook was extremely conservative. Consequently, they usually only approved art that featured the academic techniques they valued, and rejected anything that digressed from that style. Paintings were hung from the floor to the ceiling at the Salon and were crammed together across the walls. The annual opening of the exhibition was always a popular event and thousands of people bought tickets, so it was not only the walls that were crowded, but also the large halls in which the work was displayed. Another attraction was 'varnishing day', when artists were allowed in to varnish their works prior to the doors opening on the official exhibition. Even this occasion

Below: The Paris Salon. An 18th-century illustration of the Paris Salon shows how artwork was displayed. Even more was included by the 19th century.

PHOTOGRAPHY

The invention of photography in 1839 affected artists hugely. Once realistic images could be fixed on to paper without brushstrokes and the mixing of paint, the public wanted photographic portraits or views rather than paintings. Some artists gave up painting and took up photography instead; others painted even more realistically and vibrantly to show their skill over the machines. Others used photographs to liven up their compositions. Although in 1839 the painter Delaroche (1797–1859) announced, "From today, painting is dead!", many artists felt that it just had to change. It was how it was to change that caused all the conflict.

became sought after in social circles and there was a huge demand for tickets. The opportunities for artists were numerous: prominent society members and dealers would view their works as potential buyers, while journalists gave them column inches. The most alluring factor of all though, was that it was the only venue where unknown artists could exhibit their work. With his new compromising attitude, Cézanne accepted that he needed to appeal to the Salon jury – up to a point at least.

Above: Four o'clock at the Salon du Louvre, François Biard (1798–1882), 1847. Works at the Salon attracted crowds of middle-class society.

It was his only chance to make a name for himself. Narrative paintings of historical or biblical themes were the most popular items at the Salon, while Realist works were not. Although he was now involved with the group of artists who would become known as the Impressionists, Cézanne was not always in tune with their ideals. From the start, they shared beliefs, but he maintained his own ideas. Delacroix's colour palette was something that many avant-garde artists admired and copied, but Cézanne was also drawn to the imagination and expression that Delacroix incorporated in his paintings.

Below: Nadar's balloon rides. The eccentric Gaspard-Félix Tournachon (1820–1910), known as Nadar, took photographs of Paris from his hot-air balloon.

Above: Nadar's creativity with photography. In 1862, Nadar raised photography to a fine art with his aerial views of Paris, exerting a considerable influence on painters of the era.

THE SALON DES REFUSÉS

In 1863, Cézanne submitted two paintings to the Salon. They were rejected, along with an unprecedented number of works by other artists. The harsh jury maintained that it aimed to uphold the supremacy of academic art.

Cézanne expressed his fury at the jury's rejection. "I cannot accept the unjustified criticism of fellow-artists whom I have not myself expressly asked to appraise me", he complained.

A NEW KIND OF EXHIBITION
Cézanne was not the only person to react in this way; all the rejected artists were angry. Paintings turned down by the Salon jury were stamped on the back with a red 'R'. It was degrading, and discouraged potential buyers. Because of the sheer numbers of rejected artists that year, Napoleon III intervened. He created an exhibition called the Salon des Refusés, where the rebuffed artists could exhibit. The Salon attracted public ridicule at first, but it highlighted how the Salon jury selected only a particular type of painting, and it set a precedent for future independent or unofficial exhibitions. Cézanne visited it several times, along with Zola, Manet,

Above: The Artist's Studio, *Courbet, 1855. A few years before Manet arrived on the scene, Courbet shook the art world, painting ordinary people in large scale on monumental canvases.*

Pissarro, Guillaumin, James McNeill Whistler (1834–1903) and Manet. Cézanne had two pictures displayed there but they did not provoke much attention; they were not mentioned in the catalogue and remain unidentified.

MANET'S INFLUENCE
One of the most derided works on display was Manet's *Le Déjeuner sur l'Herbe*. But while the general public was scandalized by Manet's painting of a naked woman having a picnic with two fully clothed men, most of the avant-garde circle were inspired by it. Cézanne was impressed; it was the first Western painting since before the Renaissance that was intended *not* to

READY-MIXED PAINT
By the 1860s, artists were buying ready-mixed oil paints in tin tubes. Previously, painters had made their own paints when they needed them, by laboriously grinding and mixing dry pigment powders with linseed oil, and they could not be stored for very long. However, once tubes of conveniently pre-prepared paints became available, many artists began attempting to combine traditional painting methods with immediacy and spontaneity. In the 1860s, colour merchants began to include large amounts of wax with their oil-based pigments. This rendered the colours more suitable for using a palette knife for painting, a technique that had been made popular by Gustave Courbet.

be lifelike and Cézanne admired the boldness of brushwork, texture of paint and originality of composition. Manet had drawn on classical themes such as Titian's *Concert Champêtre* of c.1510, which is in the Louvre, but his sketchy application also breaks with the traditions of that style of painting. It acknowledges the Realism of Courbet. Zola became an avid supporter of Manet and of many of the forward-thinking artists exhibiting at the Salon des Refusés and wrote favourable reviews of their work in the press. The Salon des Refusés was never repeated, even though Cézanne wrote a letter to Count de Nieuwerkerke, the Director General of French museums, who held responsibility for the organization of the Paris Salon: "I want

Below: Liberty Leading the People, *Delacroix, 1830. The fluid, dramatic style and complex compositions of Delacroix, a master of Romanticism, inspired Cézanne.*

Above: Le Déjeuner sur l'Herbe, *Manet, 1862–3. Shocking the public but inspiring Cézanne and his friends, this is Manet's declaration of independence as an artist.*

Right: Young Man in the Costume of a Majo, *Manet, 1863. This was also rejected by the Salon of 1863, and demonstrates Manet's love of Spanish painting.*

to appeal to the public and have an exhibition… My wish does not seem to be at all outrageous and if you were to ask all those painters in my position, they would all reply that they rejected the jury and that they wished to take part in one way or another in an exhibition which should perforce be open to every genuine working artist."

DEVELOPING A TECHNIQUE

From that time on, Cézanne painted in an agitated style, applying pigment thickly with a palette knife and following

Delacroix's choice of palette, with emphasis on strong, deep colours such as Veronese green, yellow ochre and Prussian blue. He continued to participate in the other avant-garde artists' discussions, but his work was quite different from theirs. His realism and solid style show the influence of Courbet, and his references to the classical world reveal his admiration for both Delacroix and Manet. Yet even in his early work, before his ideas were fully formed, his understanding of underlying structures was emerging.

TORN BETWEEN TWO LIVES

By the mid-1860s, Paris had been completely and elegantly refurbished. It was now known as the 'city of light', and was worlds away from Cézanne's provincial background in Aix-en-Provence. He often moved in an attempt to find a quiet place to live in the city.

The economy of Paris was booming and its society exuded glamour and optimism. The department stores, theatre, opera, parks, cafés and restaurants were as busy in the glittering gas-lit evenings as during daylight hours.

FREQUENT RETREAT

Cézanne tried to endure Paris and concentrate on working toward his goal of creating a completely new approach to painting – one that did not derive from the expected centuries-old conventions. But the bustle of the city was still intolerable to him and he frequently moved apartments to try to find a peaceful location. He lived for a while in the rue Beautreillis on the Right Bank, and then in the rue Notre-Dame-des-Champs on the Left Bank near the Jardin du Luxembourg. When he realized that nowhere in Paris was ever completely quiet, he returned to Aix

and the tranquillity of the Jas de Bouffan (where he could save his allowance). Each year, he spent the summer in Provence, then returned to Paris

Above: Still Life of a Leg of Mutton and Bread, 1865. This is a powerful depiction of an insignificant subject.

refreshed in the winter. For the next few years, he kept up this pattern, spending part of the year in Paris and the rest mainly in Aix. For instance, in 1866, he returned to Paris in mid-February, spent a few days in July with Zola at Bennecourt, a picturesque town on the banks of the River Seine, and returned to Aix in August. While he was living in Aix, his father and his Uncle Dominique modelled for several portraits. He persuaded his uncle to dress up in various guises which he captured in powerful impasto images.

ARTISTIC DEVELOPMENT

In Provence and Paris during the 1860s, Cézanne painted portraits, landscapes and still lifes, concentrating on familiar

Left: A performance at the Académie Royale de Musique in Paris, c.1860. The glittering productions at the Paris Opéra earned Paris the name 'city of light'.

women (although in some of his letters he describes possibly platonic student love affairs). The women in his paintings and sketchbooks are often distorted, unnatural and violently painted. He was intensely shy with women, and at one point he wrote: "loneliness – that is what I am fit for". But the paintings were not necessarily born out of his inner issues; they could demonstrate his unique attempts to capture traditional themes of history. Whatever his reasons for painting them, none of these early and disturbing works were well received by the public or his friends.

THE RELUCTANT REBEL

Not surprisingly, considering his contradictory personality, Cézanne's attitude was divided between wanting to conform and attain recognition, and feeling he should rebel and help to modernize the art world. He wrote to Pissarro in 1865 that he planned to submit works to the Salon that would "make the Institute blush with rage and despair".

Below: Bread and Eggs, *1865 used dark colours, with sharp white as contrast.*

subjects with thickly applied short strokes – using a palette knife or brushes – in the robustly contrasting colours he admired in the work of Manet, Zurbarán, Courbet, Corot and Rembrandt. These works show solid subjects painted with conviction and intensity. But many of his other paintings from the second half of the 1860s are more disturbing, featuring variations on conflicts between the sexes. Much has

Above: The Cours Mirabeau, Aix-en-Provence. This is the historical centre of Aix. Even in Cézanne's day, it featured fountains, elegant homes and attractive tree-lined promenades.

been written about his reasons for painting them and theories abound about his difficulties with and fear of women. Apart from his mother and sisters, he had little contact with

PORTRAITS

Cézanne submitted work to the Salon every year from 1864 until 1869 and then most years until 1882. His work was rejected every time except the last, when one of his earlier portraits was finally accepted by the jury.

In 1882, on a friend's advice, Cézanne entered his painting, *The Artist's Father, Reading L'Événement,* which he had painted in 1866. It was his only successful submission to the Salon.

GULF OF MISUNDERSTANDING
Despite his varying styles and subjects over the years, nothing Cézanne produced changed the opinions of those in charge of the Salon. The jury continued to expect large historical scenes, images of glorious battles or noble portraits, and when confronted with his vigorous, often distorted and always unconventional works, they simply rejected them, believing that he was being facetious and mocking their ideals. Nevertheless, he continued to produce landscapes, portraits, still lifes and imaginative works, and he tried again and again, without success, to be selected for the Salon. In accordance with his contradictory personality, his aims and actions were seemingly at odds: he wanted acceptance but would never conform. Further, although his friends applauded his determination to change the traditions of art and to produce something original, they did not understand what his aspirations and intentions really were. With each submission to the Salon, a gulf of misunderstanding grew between him and the official art world.

CÉZANNE'S NEW STYLE
Academic art, as approved by the Salon jury, was produced using relatively small brushes and thin layers of paint to build up smooth surfaces and intricately realistic details. In contrast, Cézanne's working method began with thick paint that he applied with a palette knife. Using stubby marks, he created strong contrasts between whites, blacks and rich or muted colours.

Throughout the 1860s, Cézanne was always aiming to find his own style, or as he called it, a 'formula'. He spent most of his time studying

Above: Scipio, 1867. *Scipio was a regular model at the Académie Suisse. Pissarro called this painting 'a masterpiece of art'.*

Left: Portrait of Uncle Dominique, *1866. This portrait of Cézanne's uncle, a 49-year-old bailiff, is painted directly on to an unprimed canvas.*

Right: The Artist's Father, Reading 'L'Événement', 1866. *Although this was not his father's usual newspaper, Cézanne depicted Louis-Auguste reading* L'Événement *because it featured Zola's criticism of the Salon.*

the artists of the past, trying to create something original out of the work of the painters he admired.

LIFE IN AIX

In 1866, Cézanne wrote to Zola that "all pictures done inside, in the studio, will never be as good as things done in the open air". Yet during that time, few of his works were painted outside. That autumn, his former teacher Gibert invited him and his friends Baille, Marion and the journalist and critic Antony Valabrègue (1844–1900) to visit the

Left: Uncle Dominique as a Lawyer, 1866. *Cézanne painted ten portraits of his uncle in a series of guises.*

collection of old masters bequeathed to the Musée d'Aix. The works gave him further inspiration. At the same time, he began a portrait of Valabrègue. In November, Valabrègue told Zola about the rapid way Cézanne was painting: "I only posed... for one day. The uncle is usually the model. Every afternoon, another portrait appears." This brisk style changed in later years, with a more deliberate and painstaking painting process.

Although he was often in the company of the future Impressionists and agreed with many of their sentiments, he was moving in a totally different direction, revealing his independent thinking. While his friends were lightening their palettes, his choice of deep colours suggests a leaning toward Spanish painting, with methods a long way from new avant-garde styles and accepted notions of high art.

STILL LIFE

Although still life paintings had been popular for a while during the 18th century, in the hierarchy of academic genres as decreed by the official art establishment, they had been relegated to the bottom of the list.

Despite the fact that still lifes were out of favour in the 1860s, Cézanne, Manet, Henri Fantin-Latour (1836–1904) and some of the upcoming Impressionists developed an interest in the still life paintings of Jean-Baptiste-Siméon Chardin (1699–1779).

BUILDING ON TRADITION

Since the 17th century, still life painting had become relatively insignificant within the academic ranking scheme that preferred themes from history or mythology. Yet interest in Chardin, the French master of still life, was revitalized in the 1840s when Realist critics, including Jules Champfleury (1820–89) and Théophile Thoré (1807–69), wrote about him. They compared him favourably to the Realists and the Dutch 17th-century painters, as well as describing him as a courageous nonconformist who refused to paint in the fashionable Rococo style of his day. In the 1850s and 1860s, the Louvre made its first acquisitions of Chardin's works, raising his reputation even further. In the 1860s, further respected

critics published articles on Chardin's work and still life paintings became more acceptable.

Cézanne, Manet and others in their circle were eager to create something new out of this tradition and openly acknowledged their debt to past masters. During the 1860s, they helped

Above: Sugar Bowl, Pears and Blue Cup, *c.1866. In his early still lifes, Cézanne created simple, tension-filled compositions in vibrant contrasts of tone and colour.*

to revive the long-established practice of still life painting. Cézanne, Manet and Fantin-Latour (who was part of the avant-garde circle) frequently studied Chardin's work at the Louvre, and were inspired by his methods. By the 1870s, the genre had become so popular that the bourgeoisie often bought still life works and many artists supplemented their incomes by painting them.

A DIFFERENT INTERPRETATION

But Cézanne's early still lifes were not like the frank, clear works of Chardin or the colourfully detailed paintings of the Impressionists. Instead they were dark and sombre, often created with a palette knife in slabs, or with a brush in

Left: Detail from Déjeuner sur l'Herbe, *Manet, 1863. Influenced by Chardin and Courbet, Manet incorporated a traditional still life in this painting that shocked Paris.*

Above: Skull and Jug, *c.1864. Cézanne began this monochromatic work two years after he had started dividing his time between Paris and Aix.*

Below: Still Life with Skull and Candlestick, *1866. Cézanne portrayed the traditional objects of a vanitas still life, a subject filled with symbolism about the transience of life.*

comma-like swirls of impasto paint. Most of Cézanne's still lifes from that time were inspired by Chardin, but used the colours and compositions of Spanish paintings, enhanced with some of Courbet's vigour.

PARADOXES

As often happened with Cézanne, every action seemed to have an opposing reaction. So although he was influenced by still lifes of past masters, he used unorthodox new techniques to paint them, including lighting his still lifes from the front, using plenty of white paint surrounded by intense dark colours to achieve this effect. Together with his bold compositions, this created dramatic still lifes that appear calm yet powerful. Initially he painted mainly arrangements of fruit, but he gradually began to introduce other objects, all chosen for their strong and simple structures. All his still lifes are made up of carefully composed paradoxes – dark against light, straight lines alongside curves, soft textures next to hard – creating strong contrasts and tensions.

THE ENCOURAGEMENT OF FRIENDS

Zola believed that Cézanne had much more to give. He reprinted the articles he had written in *L'Événement* in a small brochure under the title *Mon Salon*, with a special preface in letter form: "To My Friend Paul Cézanne". In it, he praised their ten-year friendship. "You are my whole youth… Our minds, in their kinship, developed side by side… We turned over a mass of shocking ideas, we examined and rejected all systems, and after such strenuous labour, we told ourselves that outside of powerful and individual life there was nothing but deceit and stupidity." Despite this reassurance, Cézanne was constantly dissatisfied with his work.

Zola was not the only friend to be aware of both Cézanne's potential and his difficult moods. In 1866, his friend Marion wrote to another friend, "[Cézanne] is growing greater and greater. I truly believe that of us all it is he who will turn out to have the most violent and powerful temperament. Nevertheless he is continually discouraged."

INFLUENCES AND TENSIONS

After Zola's spirited written attempts to change the attitude of the Salon selectors,
Cézanne and his friends looked forward with interest to finding out if he had altered the
jury's opinion, and if so, what they would do the following year.

Despite Zola's impassioned appeal, unfortunately, in their stubborn and predictable way, the Salon jury and their supporting journalists were more conservative than ever in the year after his articles appeared in *L'Événement* and *Mon Salon*.

AN INSULT TO CÉZANNE

Arnold Mortier (1843–1925), a columnist at *Le Figaro*, wrote an extremely insulting piece on Cézanne, even ridiculing his name: "I have heard of two rejected paintings done by M. Sésame (nothing to do with the Arabian Nights), the same man who, in 1863, caused general mirth at the Salon des Refusés… This time M. Sésame has sent to the exhibition two compositions, which though less queer, are nevertheless just as worthy of exclusion from the Salon." Zola immediately published a reply in *Le Figaro*: "[Cézanne] was one of my childhood friends, a young painter whose strong and individual talent I respect extremely."

In 1868, perhaps the biggest insult of all came when every one of the artists in the Batignolles group except for Cézanne had work accepted for the Salon. This occurred owing to the influence of Charles-François Daubigny (1817–78), who was a friend of Monet's and who happened to be on the jury that year.

Above: Boy with a Club Foot, *Ribera, 1642. Ribera's strong composition, firm brushstrokes, earthy colours and marked tonal contrasts greatly inspired Cézanne.*

Left: Portrait of Émile Zola, *Manet, 1867–8. Zola esteemed Manet's work and wrote articles defending him against the establishment. In thanks, Manet painted this portrait, with items describing his personality, tastes and occupation.*

ODD MAN OUT

Although Cézanne often met the other artists at the Café Guerbois, he usually sat in a corner and listened, only occasionally joining in conversations. Sometimes he made his beliefs known, but more often, if the others expressed convictions that were opposed to his own, he simply got up and walked out. The others became used to his odd, irascible ways, but it did not endear him to them and most kept their distance from him. He did not share their tastes, preferring to gain inspiration from cheap fashion journals rather than the Japanese prints they admired.

ARTISTIC INSPIRATIONS

The development of a truly personal style took some time for Cézanne. He first adopted Courbet's palette-knife painting method with enthusiasm, making it integral to his style. Pissarro, like Cézanne, was always ready to experiment with a new technique such as Courbet's bold application of paint using a palette knife. But Pissarro only painted a few works using that technique, while Cézanne continued developing it for some time. In Cézanne's early imaginative works, not just Courbet,

Above: The Abduction, *1867. This painting shows the abduction of Persephone by Hades, the god of the underworld. The distortion of shape and colour serves to emphasize the drama of the event.*

but several influences came together, resulting in powerful and often disturbing paintings that blend traditional and contemporary styles. The 17th-century Spanish artist Ribera, with his scenes of violence and passion evoked with sinuous lines and strong contrasts of tone, had a strong effect on his method. Rubens' forceful approach was another big influence.

LITERARY INFLUENCES

Perhaps unexpectedly, another of Cézanne's greatest inspirations was an author and acquaintance of Zola's, Gustave Flaubert (1821–80). In the years 1857 and 1858, Flaubert's *Temptation of St Anthony* was published in instalments in the magazine *L'Artiste*. Cézanne painted some rather ambitious responses to the serial. Flaubert had recently been at the centre of a scandal over his first novel, *Madame Bovary*, which had been serialized in 1856.

Above: The Courtesans, *c.1871. Displaying the influence of painters such as Daumier and Delacroix on Cézanne, this painting also shows his transition from heavy palette-knife application to lighter brushstrokes.*

The novel's heroine conducts several adulterous affairs; the government immediately brought an action against the publisher and author on the charge of immorality, but both Flaubert and his publisher were acquitted. Cézanne was one of many people who firmly believed that Flaubert, with his combination of Romanticist and Realist styles, was one of the greatest writers of all time.

DISREGARDING THE RULES

While even the most unconventional artists who met at the Café Guerbois occasionally had work accepted by the Salon, Cézanne only experienced rejection. In response, as usual, he spent a period of isolation at his childhood home, Aix-en-Provence.

Cézanne returned to Paris in the winter of 1869, at the age of 30. He met Marie-Hortense Fiquet (1850–1922) at around the same time.

HORTENSE

By 1869, Cézanne had had little experience with women and was not yet earning a living. His friend Guillemet had managed to persuade Louis-Auguste to increase his son's allowance, so he had a little more money, but he was still completely dependent on his parents. Hortense Fiquet was a tall, brown-haired, dark-eyed 19-year-old from Saligny in the Jura. She had trained as a bookbinder but was now working

Above: Bathing on the Seine *or* La Grenouillère, Renoir, 1869. *While Cézanne was learning about the traditions of the old masters, Renoir and others were already developing an Impressionist style.*

in Paris as an artist's model. After modelling for Cézanne, Hortense moved in with him. It seems to have been a strange relationship, based on companionship rather than passion, and Cézanne kept Hortense a secret from his family. His father would never have accepted a union between his son and a girl without a dowry and she was not the sort of girl his family would expect for the heir of his father's wealth.

L'ESTAQUE AND MARSEILLES

L'Estaque is a small fishing village 50 kilometres (31 miles) west of the busy harbour town of Marseilles. During the Franco-Prussian War Marseilles was an important supply base. L'Estaque, like many places in France at the time, was in the throes of modernization, with old buildings being demolished and modern buildings and railways being erected in their place. "We must hurry, it is all disappearing," Cézanne is reputed to have said.

Right: Young Man Leaning on his Elbow, *1868. Although he was still using the traditional dark background of Spanish painters, subtle changes of structure and paint application began to emerge in Cézanne's works.*

The relationship did not affect his lifestyle much, nor his work. He continued occasionally meeting his friends at the Café Guerbois and returning periodically to Aix, and he carried on painting just as before. Although she was a ready and patient model, she did not appreciate his work and he described her as liking only "Paris and lemonade". Within a few months of their meeting (after he had witnessed Zola's marriage in May), Cézanne was back in Aix.

THE FRANCO-PRUSSIAN WAR

In July 1870, when the Franco-Prussian War broke out, Cézanne was still in Aix. To avoid being called up, he hid at first in the Jas de Bouffan, but when the gendarmes came looking for him, he escaped to the small fishing village of L'Estaque, close to Marseilles in southern France. His mother had rented a fisherman's house there and for the duration of the war he hid in L'Estaque with Hortense. When his call-up papers were sent to him, he simply

ignored them. He later wrote: "During the war I did a lot of painting in the open air at L'Estaque. But I have nothing exceptional to report about 1870–1. I divided my time between landscapes and studio work."

PAINTING IN THE OPEN AIR

While he was staying in L'Estaque, Cézanne discovered the pleasure of painting views from his window and around the village, capturing the changes in the seasons. He responded

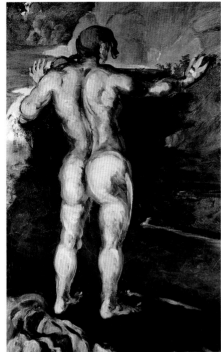

Above: Bather and Rocks, *1867–9. This expressive work anticipated many 20th-century styles of painting. Nothing like this had been seen before.*

by studying the forces of nature in greater detail and by painting in the open air more often. A subtle difference occurred in his painting style from that time. His close depiction of nature became more important and he began to concentrate mainly on landscapes and still lifes, painting with shorter and more varied brush marks. He was attempting to create something more enduring than an exact rendition of what he saw before him, and his focus on underlying structures became an all-consuming passion. His work became more controlled and his fresh approach to nature was unlike anything the other progressive artists were doing, even though they too were responding to nature. He began looking for the truth that lay beneath appearances, and through this approach, he was able to restrain and channel his inner conflicts.

Left: The Avenue at the Jas de Bouffan, *1871. Cropped at the top with thick stripes of greens and browns to evoke an impression of depth, this avenue of chestnut trees was one of Cézanne's favourite themes.*

FURTHER REJECTION

Although he was working in L'Estaque at the time, rather than Paris, and hiding himself away to avoid conscription, and despite past disappointments, Cézanne optimistically submitted a couple of recent paintings to the Salon of 1870.

It seems odd that Cézanne expected to have his paintings accepted by the jury, after all the years of conflict between him and the Salon before this, but this year, once more, he felt hopeful.

IRRECONCILABLE DIFFERENCES

Almost inevitably, Cézanne's works were rejected. Within a short time a scathing cartoon was printed in the press, featuring a malicious caricature of him with a drooping moustache, surrounded by his rejected works. Maintaining his defiant attitude, he wrote to the cartoonist, a Mr Stock: "Yes, my dear Mr Stock, I paint how I

Above: The Clearing, *1867. This painting is softer than many previous works and contains more colours. It is beginning to show the influence of Impressionist ideas.*

see, how I feel – and I have very strong feelings. Other people also feel and see as I do, but they do not take risks. Well, I take risks, my good man, I have the courage of my opinions and he who laughs last, laughs longest." From that time on, the relationship between Cézanne and the Paris Academy became irrevocably damaged. His contempt of them had reached an all-time high and their disapproval of him

was deeper than ever. Yet to modern eyes, it is clear that by this time, his style was moving toward maturity. His economy of line and colour is indicative of his growing interest in understanding and depicting the essence of everything around him. He was beginning to move away from trying only to create three-dimensional illusions on two-dimensional surfaces and to explore other ways to represent the physical world on canvas.

THE POST-WAR WORLD

In January 1871, as the Franco-Prussian War came to an end, the French authorities were actively seeking Cézanne for evading conscription, but when the armistice was signed in February, the matter was dropped. Unrest continued in Paris, so Cézanne and Hortense remained in Provence for awhile. In the early summer Cézanne

THE COMMUNE

After the surrender of Paris to the Prussians in January 1871, a French National Assembly was elected to negotiate the peace. But the first president of the National Assembly stopped paying the National Guards and began claiming taxes from the people. By March, hundreds of discontented and disillusioned Parisians rose up in revolt and organized their own revolutionary government, which they called the Commune of Paris. They used a red flag as their symbol and declared that they wanted a democratic and social republic. A civil war broke out between the Commune and the government troops and after just two months of power, the Commune was crushed.

Right: The Strangled Woman, *1875–6. Many critics of this painting describe it as showing Cézanne's misogyny, but this is possibly an exercise in Romantic drama.*

Above: Damaged Royal Palace of the Tuileries in Paris, *photograph, 1871. The ruins of the Royal Palace are shown after it had been damaged and burned during the Commune insurrection of May 1871.*

went to the Jas de Bouffan and spent most of his time painting as he always did. Without his knowledge, he had been made a committee member by the new town council in Aix and he was asked to supervise the art school and museum there. But he was never interested in civic affairs and he chose not to become involved, preferring to devote himself to painting, as often as possible in solitude.

RETURN TO PARIS

After the troubles, in the late summer of 1871, Cézanne returned to Paris. Hortense was pleased to be back – and she was expecting a baby. Cézanne's friend Achille Emperaire stayed with him for a few months, but Cézanne's moods made it difficult and Emperaire soon moved out. Although dissatisfied with his inability to support his mistress, Cézanne was still determined to create art that mattered.

Right: The Pastoral or Idyll, *1870. This ambiguous work refers back to Manet's* Le Déjeuner sur l'Herbe.

PISSARRO AT PONTOISE

On 4 January 1872, Cézanne and Hortense's son Paul was born in Paris. Although he was delighted with his son, Cézanne's feelings of loneliness persisted and he feared that his father might find out about his mistress and child.

Cézanne was beset by financial problems, and worried about how to introduce Hortense and the new baby to his family. Inevitably, his mood darkened. Luckily, at this point, Pissarro invited him to stay in Pontoise.

ESCAPE FROM PARIS

Pontoise is in the Oise Valley, 28 kilometres (18 miles) from Paris. Cézanne took his family there in the autumn of 1872, and they stayed in a hotel near Pissarro's apartment. He was pleased to be with Pissarro, who, in their ten years of friendship, had never failed in his conviction that Cézanne had extraordinary potential. He was

relieved to experience a change of air with someone who believed that his work mattered, and to escape from the fear of his father discovering his secret. Pissarro, who was more mature and patient, began to advise Cézanne, guiding him away from his dark and dramatic early style and advising the integration of some of the future Impressionists' ideas. Although Cézanne had dismissed these ideas when they discussed them at the Café Guerbois, Pissarro's eagerness to try out new approaches helped Cézanne to see things from different perspectives and to appreciate some of the notions he had rebuffed. Pissarro, impressed by the younger artist's work, said of him: "He'll surprise many an artist who has written him off too soon."

Above: Cézanne and Pissarro, 1877. Cézanne is sitting on the bench in Pissarro's garden at Pontoise and Pissarro, with the white beard, is standing.

Below: Village near Pontoise, Pissarro, 1873. Pissarro's brushwork formed hatched parallel patterns on his warm and cool, and light and dark areas.

PAINTING
EN PLEIN AIR

Before the mid-19th century, landscape artists would make sketches outside in all weathers and all seasons, but they almost always completed their work in the studio. Once paint became sold in portable tin tubes, painting *en plein air* (in the open air), directly from nature, became possible and was an important aspect of landscape painting. Advocates believed that being outside, looking directly at the source, was the only way to capture a true likeness, even though it might be sketchier than studio work. The *plein air* tradition had started with the English landscapists and painters of the Barbizon school, followed by the Realists and then the Impressionists, when it became central to their aspiration of capturing the effects of light (although most artists still finished their paintings in their studios).

CHANGING STYLE

Cézanne and Pissarro often went out to paint in the countryside, and other artists joined them. Away from Paris, Cézanne relaxed. He became familiar with Pissarro's methods and ideas and he even copied one of Pissarro's paintings of Louveciennes to gain an insight into his technique. Pissarro criticized Cézanne's harsh outlines and his flat areas of paint applied with palette knives, suggesting that he should consider softer gradations of tone and smaller paint marks. He encouraged Cézanne to paint only what he saw in front of him, to observe nature directly and objectively, moving away from heavy, theatrical themes. They both gained from each other's company. Cézanne brightened his palette, differentiated more gradually between tones, and put aside his large palette knives to apply small brush marks, featuring dabs and touches of lighter colour. His canvases became more harmonious and he paid closer attention to aerial perspective. Under Cézanne's influence, Pissarro's works gained a firmer structure.

Right: The Road at Pontoise, 1875. From his time with Pissarro, Cézanne began painting reality as he saw it, without embellishment or interpretation.

The picturesque surroundings of Pontoise gave Cézanne time for reflection. He said to Pissarro: "I see superb things and I need to decide to paint solely *en plein air.*" His work did not change radically, but the subtle differences reveal how educational the time with Pissarro was for him. Pissarro was delighted to see Cézanne's style blossom, but he was too modest to take the credit for it. Cézanne, however,

Above: June Morning near Pontoise, Pissarro, 1873. Using characteristically small, angled brush marks, Pissarro explores the effects of light and colour.

acknowledged Pissarro's influence and often referred to it. For a long time, Cézanne thought of himself as Pissarro's pupil, describing him as "like a father to me, rather like the good Lord". He also said, "We all stem from Pissarro."

AUVERS-SUR-OISE

Through Pissarro, Cézanne met Dr Paul Gachet (1828–1909), a physician who believed in both conventional and alternative medicine, and who was also an amateur painter with a great interest in new developments in art.

Dr Gachet admired Courbet and Manet, empathized with the avant-garde artists and was happy to accept artworks from artist patients who were unable to pay his fees at his private practice in Paris.

A NEW ADMIRER

Dr Gachet occasionally went to the Café Guerbois, which is how he came to know several of the progressive artists and writers of the day. In 1872, he bought a house in Auvers-sur-Oise, not far from Pontoise, where he lived for three days a week with his wife and two children, returning to his practice in Paris to work on the other days. He already knew Pissarro, and it was through him that he came to meet Cézanne. He admired Cézanne's work from the moment he saw it. When he discovered Cézanne's situation, in his extremely open-minded manner he set about persuading him to move Hortense and the baby from the hotel in which they were staying and to live with him and his wife in Auvers. Not many people in the doctor's situation would have welcomed an unmarried mother, an illegitimate child and an almost penniless painter into their home, but from February 1873 until the spring of 1874, Cézanne, Hortense and the baby stayed at Dr Gachet's house in the small village of Auvers.

Above right: The Village Road, Auvers, *c.1872–3. Cézanne's palette had not yet lightened significantly, but this painting shows fewer strong contrasts than his earlier work.*

Right: Landscape, Auvers, *c.1873. Working with Pissarro, Cézanne moved closer to the Impressionist style, painting from nature, but he still retained a more structured composition and a sober atmosphere.*

Dr Gachet had converted the attic of his house into a studio, where he, Cézanne, Pissarro and Guillaumin, who had been with Cézanne at the Académie Suisse and who also frequented the Café Guerbois, produced etchings. For Cézanne, Auvers was close enough to Pontoise to make painting with Pissarro practicable, and its proximity to Paris meant other artists also visited. The eccentricities of Dr Gachet appealed to him and the two men found they had a wealth of topics to debate.

ARTISTIC DEVELOPMENT

Cézanne spent his time painting around Auvers, exploring the changes that occurred in nature throughout the seasons. As well as these landscape paintings and etchings made in the studio, he also painted still lifes of Mme Gachet's flower-filled Delft vases. One of his first images of Auvers was of Dr Gachet's house, and in that painting, as in most of his landscapes of that time, he borrowed his composition style from Pissarro. Pissarro in turn had been influenced by Corot and by photography. Most of Cézanne's paintings feature gently curving lines from the foreground to the background, drawing viewers' eyes into and around the scenes. But his paintings were still more solid than the developing Impressionists' style. Rather than using flickering, angled brushwork, he built up blocks of colour and tone. As he never sought to capture just the effects of light, but always tried to create a more solid effect, his approach was more complex than theirs; however, he concurred with their interest in colour and light. His work of that time shows a mixture of styles. His dark swathes of colour had disappeared; his narrative and allegorical themes had been almost completely abandoned; his palette was brighter and his application lighter.

A COMFORTABLE LIFE

Cézanne was probably at his most relaxed and comfortable during that period. Having three admirers around him must have helped: the intelligent and thoughtful Dr Gachet; Guillaumin, who had declared that he was a greater painter than Manet; and Pissarro, who believed he had the potential for genius. He was also delighted with his son and felt at ease away from Paris. He confided in his mother about Hortense and the baby, but kept his father in the dark for fear of provoking his wrath. His allowance was, after all, the only money he had with which to support his family.

Above: Well Driller, *1873–5. Cézanne painted this oil study of a workman in Auvers during his time living there. His approach shows some of his former style with newer ideas emerging.*

Left: Dr Gachet's House, Auvers, *1873. This tall white house features in several of Cézanne's early views of Auvers. Pissarro's influence can be seen in the composition and approach.*

THE BATIGNOLLES GROUP

The need for natural light meant that artists usually had to stop working at dusk. All over Paris, they would put down their brushes and chisels and gather in one of the many cafés set up in the newly glittering capital.

The artists and writers who did not conform to the accepted academic styles met regularly at the Café Guerbois from 1866 to 1875. They debated their new ideas and discussed their frustration with the establishment that labelled them 'les bohèmes' (the bohemians).

OVERCOMING ISOLATION

Once they had met their friends – at least two days a week, on Thursdays and Sundays – the rest of the late afternoon and evening would be spent sitting around marble-topped tables, discussing their aims and exchanging opinions. Initially, Manet went to the Café de Bade at 23 boulevard des Italiens, but in 1864 he moved to an apartment on the boulevard des Batignolles, closer to Baudelaire, Bazille, Fantin-Latour, Pissarro, Renoir and later Cézanne. By 1866, they had started frequenting the Café Guerbois. Soon others joined them, including Zola, the novelist and art critic Louis Edmond

Above: A Studio at Les Batignolles, *Fantin-Latour, 1870. The artist Fantin-Latour quietly observed the group that gathered around Manet and painted them as serious, respectable figures.*

Duranty (1833–80), Guillemet, Degas, etcher and printmaker Félix Bracquemond (1833–1914), poet and critic Armand Silvestre (1837–1901), Monet, Sisley and Dr Gachet. They became known as the Batignolles group.

PASSIONATE DEBATE

The conversations among the group in the café were often intense and heated; occasional fallings-out occurred, and in early 1870 there was even a duel between Manet and Duranty. But in the main, they were of one accord and were all great friends. Monet later recalled, "Nothing could have been more stimulating than the regular discussions which we used to have there, with their constant clashes of

Above: Émile Zola (1840–1902) Reading, *1881–4. Cézanne made this pencil sketch of his old friend at the time they often met at the Café Guerbois in Paris.*

opinion. They kept our wits sharpened … and kept us going until the final realization of an idea was accomplished." They were drawn together in their search for new forms of expression and the need to overcome feelings of isolation that could so easily have engulfed each of them in the face of rejection from the official artistic quarters. The Salon often exercised its authority and rejected their work, keeping them from exhibiting. After the Franco-Prussian War, they began to form an idea. Strongly believing that they were creating art of real value, they felt certain that through exhibiting their work, they would be able to overcome the public's lack of understanding.

THE ANONYMOUS SOCIETY OF ARTISTS

The growing sense of common purpose between the artists of the Batignolles group resulted in their forming the Société Anonyme des Artistes, Peintres, Sculpteurs et Graveurs (The Anonymous Society of Artists, Painters, Sculptors and Engravers). From the start, Cézanne was involved with the society. Their primary aim was to mount independent group exhibitions free from selection by a jury. In 1873, the group decided to arrange their own exhibition, even though this would be controversial and expensive. They did not intend to promote any particular style of art, but simply to invite people to see and appreciate their work, and they set about finding a venue for their exhibition.

Above: Cézanne's Accessories, 1873. Although some of the darkest tones are still strong, Cézanne has now lightened his palette and used more delicate brushwork than in previous paintings.

Below: Portrait of Cézanne, Pissarro, 1874. When Cézanne was staying at Auvers-sur-Oise, near Pontoise, Pissarro produced several etchings of him in Dr Gachet's attic studio.

PÈRE TANGUY

In 1873, Julien Tanguy (1825–93) was released from prison in Brest, where he had been incarcerated for participating in the Commune. By trade, he was an artist's colourman and a painter, and he became friends with many of the Batignolles group. As soon as he was freed, he opened a small art shop in the rue Clauzel in Montmartre. In no time, the shop became another vital haunt for artists of the Batignolles group. When they could not afford to pay, Tanguy accepted their paintings and drawings in exchange for materials; he also acted as a dealer and patron for them.

IMPORTANT MEETING

When Cézanne met him in December 1873, 'Père' Tanguy, as he became known, immediately supported him. He took several of Cézanne's canvases, allowing Cézanne to select art materials he needed in exchange. Although Cézanne was trying to support a family of three on his allowance, Tanguy encouraged him to carry on painting.

SENSATION

In 1874, the Société Anonyme des Artistes, Peintres, Sculpteurs et Graveurs found
a venue for their first exhibition: they decided to use the photographer Nadar's studio
at 35 boulevard des Capucines. The critics were scathing about Cézanne's work.

When Pissarro invited Cézanne to exhibit, there was an outcry among other members of the Society. They believed that his work would upset visitors, and Manet, who had been intending to send some paintings, immediately withdrew.

INDEPENDENT ART EXHIBITION

The idea of an exhibition separate from the Salon had been brewing since 1867, but it was not only contentious, it would also be costly for the artists involved. Yet as a number of the artists were beginning to sell their paintings and sculptures through some collectors, they believed that their work was potentially popular. They discussed the idea and worked out all the details, and eventually, the independent exhibition of the Société Anonyme des Artistes, Peintres, Sculpteurs et Graveurs opened on 15 April 1874 at Nadar's studio. It lasted one month. Along with the Batignolles group, more conventional artists who merely wanted to avoid the selection process of the Salon exhibited their work. Yet the revolutionary artists bore the brunt of the criticism. They included Renoir, Monet, Pissarro, Sisley, Guillaumin, Degas and Berthe Morisot (1841–95). Manet, who had withdrawn because of Cézanne, said: "[Cézanne is] a bricklayer who paints with his trowel". In total, 30 artists displayed 165 works, including three paintings by Cézanne. His works were: *The House of the Hanged Man, Auvers-sur-Oise* (1872–3), *A Modern Olympia* (c.1873) and *Landscape at Auvers* (c.1873).

CRITICISM AND SUCCESS

With its predominance of bright colours, swift brushwork and contemporary subject matter, the exhibition generated hilarity and censure among the public, but by the end of the month, 3,500 visitors had attended and the Salon system had been considerably weakened – suddenly it was not the only way for an

Left: Self-portrait, 1875. Cézanne created several self-portraits during the course of his life. All are painted without flattery or emotion.

Above: Nadar's studio, 1874. The central position of 35 boulevard des Capucines in Paris was an excellent spot for the first exhibition of the independent artists.

Left: A Modern Olympia, c.1873–4. *Inspired by Manet's shocking painting* Olympia *of 1863, Cézanne included a self-portrait in this work, which he painted as a gift for Dr Gachet.*

On another positive note, Cézanne had one of his first successes: Count Doria (1824–96), a wealthy financier and collector of contemporary painting, bought *The House of the Hanged Man* for 300 francs.

DIFFERENCES OF OPINION

A month after the exhibition closed, Cézanne returned to Aix, leaving Hortense and Paul in Paris. As usual he got on well with his mother and sister Marie, but continued to clash with his father over his choice of career. He had asked his father to increase his allowance to 200 francs a month, but Louis-Auguste was not co-operative. Additionally, Cézanne's former tutor Gibert asked to see his work, having read about it in the papers. On viewing the work, a horrified Gibert turned and walked away.

Below: The House of the Hanged Man, *1873. Demonstrating Cézanne's 'Impressionist phase', this work shows Pissarro's influence with its use of light and delicate, dabbing brushwork.*

artist's work to be viewed. Cézanne's work was particularly scorned. Critics smirked at how naturalism was already showing 'regrettable signs of decay' and succumbing to 'unrestrained Romanticism where Nature is merely a pretext for reveries'. One reviewer ridiculed *A Modern Olympia*: "On Sunday, the public had occasion to scoff at a fantastic figure being presented to a dope addict beneath opium heavens.

This apparition of naked, delicate pink flesh, a sensual incubus – this little hideaway in some fabricated paradise astounded even the most daring. M. Cézanne gives the impression of being a species of lunatic, painting with delirium tremens." Cézanne was hurt by the scathing reviews, but the artists felt that they had been seen as painters who were serious about their work and not merely trying to ridicule the Salon.

IMPRESSIONISM

The term 'Impressionism' was coined from the independent exhibition of 1874. Few reviewers took any of the work seriously, and one of Monet's paintings, *Impression, Sunrise*, where he had expressly captured the sensation of an early morning, showed, through sketchy brushwork and thin paint, the atmosphere rather than the details of a scene. The critic Louis Leroy derided the work in a satirical review entitled 'The Exhibition of the Impressionists', declaring that "wallpaper in its embryonic state is more finished than that seascape". In due course, the nickname stuck.

VICTOR CHOCQUET

Despite the derision most of their works had generated, the Impressionists were eager to keep showing their art publicly. Unfortunately many of them were in dire straits financially, so some auctioned their works in the Hôtel Drouot.

It was not practicable to organize another exhibition the following year as the artists were unable to meet the costs, so holding the auction was an alternative. It was here that Cézanne acquired an influential patron.

THE AUCTION

The Hôtel Drouot opened in the early 1850s and was the main auction house in Paris. It was close to the stock exchange and in the same street as the major banks. In 1875, Monet, Morisot, Renoir and Sisley auctioned their work there, but instead of bidding, the people at the auction jeered and heckled the auctioneer so much that the police were called in. The 73 works offered for sale only realized 11,496 francs in total; Renoir was even forced to buy several of his own works to prevent them from selling too cheaply. But as a result of the sale, Victor Chocquet (1821–91), an inspector with the Paris Customs Service who had his own private means, commissioned Renoir to paint portraits of himself and his wife. He was deeply impressed by the work he had seen. The two men got on extremely well and Renoir decided to introduce Chocquet to the work of his friends. Recognizing that Cézanne would find it more difficult to attract patronage than the rest of them, Renoir took Chocquet first to Père Tanguy's shop to show him Cézanne's paintings. At that time, Cézanne was living on the quai d'Anjou, next to Guillaumin. The two occasionally painted together around Paris, but he still had fewer friends than the others in the group and spent a great deal of time on his own.

Top right: Five Bathers, *1876–7. Cézanne's studies of bathers became a personal theme, not prompted by classical ideals but by coarse realism.*

Above: Portrait of Victor Chocquet, *1875–7. With an Impressionist-style paint application, Cézanne's portrait of his patron is reminiscent of El Greco's attenuated figures.*

Above: Self-portrait with a Casquette, *c.1872. Cézanne's free brushstrokes are both immediate and expressive. He looks older than his 33 years, possibly owing to his inner turmoil.*

PATRONAGE

Chocquet had not seen the Impressionists' work before, and when he saw it for the first time at the Hôtel Drouot, he admired it immensely. He had been advised against going to the independent exhibition the previous year by friends. On seeing Cézanne's work at Père Tanguy's, he was overwhelmed. He immediately bought a painting, exclaiming: "How nice this will look between a Delacroix and a Courbet." Through Renoir, he invited Cézanne to his apartment on the rue de Rivoli and showed him his Delacroix watercolours (he owned almost 20 of these as well as works by Manet and Courbet). For once, Cézanne forgot to be awkward and self-conscious, and enthused eloquently about Delacroix, one of his favourite painters. The two men recognized similar opinions in each other and became friends. Chocquet commissioned a portrait from him and Cézanne painted two. Now Cézanne had patronage and support from Gachet, Tanguy and Chocquet. Although they did not buy many works, nor did they pay high prices for them, at least they liked them enough to pay something, which was encouraging. As the first collector to recognize Cézanne's genius, Chocquet gave him a fair price and supported him when critics became especially hostile. He never tired of praising Cézanne's work to others, believing him to be one of the greatest living painters. Many were amused by this and considered Chocquet to be mildly insane.

CÉZANNE AND IMPRESSIONISM

Throughout 1875, Cézanne continued accommodating the Impressionistic styles he had learned from Pissarro, applying small brush marks and using varying shades and tonal contrasts to convey the play of light on objects. The following summer, he went to L'Estaque to paint some seascapes and views of the Gulf of Marseilles that Chocquet had commissioned. He wrote to Pissarro from there: "I have started painting what Monsieur Chocquet asked for, two small pictures with the sea in the background. It's like a playing card here. Red roofs against a blue sea… there are compositions which would take three to four months' work, which could probably be done because the vegetation doesn't change. The olive and pine trees always keep their leaves."

Below: The Étang des Soeurs, Osny, near Pontoise, c.1875. Once he had assumed a more Impressionist style, Cézanne used smaller palette knives with more delicate application, establishing strong diagonal rhythms in the foliage.

BRIGHT, DAZZLING LIGHT

Cézanne did not participate in the second Impressionist exhibition in April 1876.
Instead of remaining in Paris, in the spring of 1876, he went to Provence, where
he continued developing his own independent style.

Cézanne was disheartened by his first experience of exhibiting his work and did not want to be the butt of the critics once again.

STRIVING AFTER PERFECTION

Despite Cézanne's difficulties in gaining recognition, and the hostility he attracted from the press and the official art world, his confidence in his work was increasing. In a letter to his mother in 1874, he wrote of this growing self-assurance: "I am beginning to consider myself stronger than all those around me and you know that the good opinion I have of myself has only been reached after serious consideration. I have to work all the time… I must strive after perfection only for the satisfaction of becoming truer and wiser."

The landscapes he painted during the middle years of the 1870s demonstrate how he was trying to reach perfection. His technique had changed from his earlier swathes of paint and subjective elements to a

more objective interpretation of what he saw before him, using a series of controlled daubs and patches of colour that suggest the play of light on elements in the scene. For the first time

Above: Life in the Fields, *1876–7. This colourful narrative painting, worked in a soft, sketchy style, features five figures and some animals in an idyllic country scene.*

since he began painting, his style became less restricted, and many of his marks remained unblended on his canvases. These paintings are no longer as heavy as his earlier works – they are the softest and most Impressionistic of his career. He had become interested in the clarity of the light in Provence, and rendered its strong contrasts and sharply defined forms in bright colours and layers of paint. Unlike the Impressionists, he was still striving to attain a style that would embody all his philosophies, while most of the other artists had already established their own style.

Left: The Temptation of St Anthony, *c.1877. Cézanne was inspired by Flaubert, whose version of* The Temptation of St Anthony *had been serialized in 1874, but he was now painting far fewer of these imaginary scenes.*

Right: Pissarro and Cézanne in 1875. While Cézanne did not make friends readily, when he did forge a friendship, it was usually strong and lasting.

SUMMER IN L'ESTAQUE

In the summer of 1876, spending time in L'Estaque to paint Chocquet's paintings, he was exhilarated by the bright, dazzling light. He wrote to Pissarro: "The landscape here would suit you marvellously… The sun is so tremendous that it seems to me as if the objects were silhouetted not only in black and white, but in blue, red, brown and violet." This explains how he was moving away from his Impressionistic interlude. With firm marks and an intensely coloured palette, he constructed strong compositions with diagonal, horizontal and vertical lines depicting the bay, the sea, trees and land masses. His application of paint, whether using smaller palette knives or thinner brushes, was thick, assured and systematic. Unlike the Impressionists' style, he worked slowly and deliberately. Rather than contrasts of light, he described forms with inflections of colour.

Below: The Fishermen (Fantastic Scene), c.1875. This work demonstrates how Cézanne was interpreting a mix of Manet, Monet, Giorgione, Titian and Veronese in a particularly brightened palette.

DEVELOPING A UNIQUE STYLE

Cézanne never abandoned any technique until he was sure that it was not going to be useful to him. Thus in several of the paintings in L'Estaque that year, the Impressionistic manner is still apparent, with a pronounced naturalism and soft gradations of colour and tone. Foliage, sea and other elements were often built up with luminous tones and a delicate touch, showing that he was still using Impressionists' methods while constructing his own approach. Cézanne kept his options open until he knew that a technique could be discarded.

CONQUERING PARIS WITH AN APPLE

Toward the end of the 1870s, Cézanne began evolving a method of applying paint to his canvases, which became known as his 'constructive' style. His more sophisticated compositions and the lighter palette of this period show that he had learned much from his time in Pontoise and was using this to develop uniquely and independently. But he was still a long way from reaching an approach that satisfied him and he recognized how different his ideas were from other avant-garde artists around him.

Above: Still Life with Milk Jug and Fruit, c.1900.
Left: Still Life with Vase of Flowers, c.1883–5.

THE THIRD EXHIBITION

In 1877, although they were still struggling financially, the Impressionists organized their third independent exhibition. This time it was held in a private apartment at 6 rue Le Peletier, from 4 April to 30 April.

Only 18 artists participated in the third Paris exhibition in 1877, compared with 19 in 1876 and 30 in 1874. A total of 241 works were exhibited, including 16 by Cézanne.

GUSTAVE CAILLEBOTTE

It was largely owing to the generosity of Gustave Caillebotte (1848–94) that the third exhibition took place. Caillebotte had a law degree and was also an engineer, but he had studied painting since the end of the Franco-Prussian War and had been involved with the organization of the Impressionists' first exhibition in 1874. He had made his debut as a painter in the second exhibition of 1876, in which his realist style of Impressionism was favourably received. With his large independent income, he could afford to finance a number of aspects of the third exhibition, including the five-roomed apartment rented for the event and the extensive advance publicity the

Above: Bathers at Rest, *c.1876. This is a sketch for a final painting of the same name. The short, jabbing brushstrokes are probably inspired by Courbet's style.*

Impressionists produced, although he was to be reimbursed out of the admission charges.

CÉZANNE'S CONTRIBUTION

Pissarro had set up an alternative group to the Impressionists called L'Union, along with a minor painter and part-time art dealer, Alfred Meyer. Cézanne and Guillaumin had joined the group. L'Union was holding a rival independent

Left: Still Life: Flask, Glass and Jug, *c.1877. Every small dab of paint represents space, light and structure. He had understood Impressionism, and now Cézanne began to establish his own style.*

exhibition from 15 February 1877 at the Grand Hotel on the boulevard des Capucines, in the same street where the first Impressionist exhibition was held. But just before it opened, Cézanne, Pissarro and Guillaumin opted out of L'Union, choosing instead to exhibit with the Impressionists in April, and consequently L'Union's exhibition was a complete flop. It is not known whether Cézanne sought his father's permission to exhibit with the Impressionists or whether he simply decided that he would take the risk in the hope that his work would sell. He showed three watercolours, over a dozen still lifes and landscapes and a portrait of Victor Chocquet.

THE CRITICS

More visitors attended this exhibition than either of the previous shows – in all, about 8,000 people passed through the doors. Yet if anything, the critics were even more scathing toward Cézanne. He was described as 'intransigent, stubborn, pigheaded, fantastic', and Leroy, who had originally dubbed the artists Impressionists, urged pregnant women to hurry past his portrait of Chocquet: "This strange, leathery head might make too powerful an impression on you and cast a spell on the fruit of your wombs, infecting it with jaundice before it sees the light of day."

All the artists had hoped to be met with more respect at this exhibition, and the hostility and hilarity were hard to bear. Chocquet, who attended every day, was incensed at the vituperative comments about Cézanne's work. He moved about the exhibition, challenging each group, vigorously expounding the virtues of Cézanne's work and trying to make the visitors ashamed. But he simply amused them even more and added to his reputation as a madman.

THE SUPPORTERS

For the duration of the exhibition, 22-year-old Georges Rivière, who was a friend of Renoir, published a small paper called L'Impressioniste, defending the exhibitors. He wrote most of the articles himself, with a few contributions by Renoir, and explained that the artists

Above: Landscape near Paris, c.1876. *Featuring shades of emerald which were soon to be characteristic of his palette, this is one of Cézanne's most obviously Impressionistic landscapes.*

had adopted the name 'Impressionists' to clarify the difference between their work and academic art. He particularly praised Cézanne. His writing, however, was amateurish, and his connection

Above: Bather Sitting at the Water's Edge, 1876. *Cézanne's bathers are one of his recurring themes. They always avert their eyes and often appear distorted.*

with the Impressionists was too obvious for him to be taken seriously. "M. Cézanne", he wrote, "as an artist is like a Greek of the classical period."

Zola also wrote a review of the exhibition. He described Monet as "the outstanding personality among the exhibitors", and then continued: "Next I wish to name M. Paul Cézanne, who is certainly the greatest colourist of the group. There are, in the exhibition, some Provençal landscapes of his which have a splendid character. The canvases of this painter, so strong and so deeply felt, may cause the bourgeois to smile, but they nevertheless contain the makings of a great artist."

CONTINUING STRUGGLES

Cézanne was depressed and frustrated over the public humiliations at the third independent exhibition, and he became more insular and withdrawn. He realized that he was approaching 40 years old, and was still in dire financial straits.

COLOUR THEORIES

Plein air painting and colour theories were the only two technical characteristics that all the Impressionists (except Degas) and Cézanne had in common. Even when he moved away from their style, he retained a fascination for colour and an interest in the theories of scientists such as Eugène Chevreul (1786–1889). These theories were concerned mainly with the optical effects of combinations and contrasts, and with the juxtapositions of the primary, secondary and complementary colours.

Above: Portrait of Hortense, c.*1877. Hortense Fiquet, Cézanne's mistress, posed for many watercolour and oil portraits and featured in other works, including* A Modern Olympia, c.*1873–4.*

Cézanne decided not to participate in any further Impressionist exhibitions. The other artists asked him to continue, but he decided instead to focus on being accepted at the Salon.

Above: Madame Cézanne in a Red Armchair, c.*1877. Painted just before the third Impressionist exhibition, this picture shows how Cézanne built up rich contrasts to create a tapestry-like effect.*

COMPARISONS WITH OTHERS

In 1877, Zola achieved financial and social success with the publication of his novel *L'Assommoir,* which was part of a series of 20 books. Assured of his continuing popularity, he became one of the highest paid contemporary French writers, and was sought after in fashionable literary and social circles. Among Cézanne's artist friends, Monet had attracted several loyal collectors and Renoir was experiencing a new surge of success. In 1879, one of his canvases was exhibited at the Salon and sold for 1,000 francs. Even Pissarro was beginning to sell his work quite regularly to a growing following.

A DARK YEAR

In stark contrast, Cézanne's work was still not selling, except to Tanguy and Chocquet, and he owed Tanguy 2,174 francs for artists' materials. Then things became even worse. On 20 March 1878, his father intercepted a letter from Cézanne to Chocquet, revealing the existence of Hortense and their six-year-old illegitimate son. Hypocritically ignoring the fact that his own son and one of his daughters were also born illegitimate, Louis-Auguste was furious. He had retired from his bank after the Franco-Prussian War and had transferred his assets to his three children so that they would avoid paying inheritance tax, but he still had complete control of his money, and now that his son had disappointed him in every respect, he halved his allowance. In desperation, Cézanne wrote to Zola asking if he could find him a job. Zola began sending Hortense monthly payments of 60 francs.

The humiliation continued. In Aix, Cézanne's relationship with his father was at an all-time low, and he also discovered that locals treated him as an oddity since word had spread about his incomprehensible work. Even schoolboys jeered at him. That April, the Salon accepted a painting by Renoir, but once again, Cézanne's work was rejected.

NEW PAINTING TECHNIQUES

Cézanne had always believed that Impressionism was too ephemeral and lacked structure. Rather than simply depicting superficial appearances, he was more interested in capturing hidden aspects of the structure of each object he painted. He also preferred to focus on colour more than light. In his quest to concentrate on underlying structures, from July 1878 to March 1879 he worked in L'Estaque, developing a new method of distributing colour across his canvases, without including any specific light source. Instead of the curving brushstrokes of his earlier works, he began applying straight marks in an almost patchwork style, building up suggestions of structure, depth and

Right: Roofs, 1877. This is one of Cézanne's few townscapes; the idea of painting roofs probably came from looking at Pissarro's work.

space with overlapping layers of vivid hues. In this way, colour became the most important element of his paintings. He avoided strong sunlight, only going out to paint when the light was more diffused. He said: "There is a logic of colour; the painter owes obedience to this alone and never to the logic of the intellect. He must always follow the logic of his eyes." At first, unlike the Impressionists, he began using a comparatively wide palette, consisting of five yellows, six reds, three greens and three blues as well as black and white. He declared: "Every form change is a colour change."

Below: Le Buffet (The sideboard), 1877–9. Although he touched on Impressionist ideas, Cézanne always emphasized the solidity and permanence of forms, focusing on spatial unity.

MOVING TO MELUN

While Hortense and Paul were living in Marseilles, Cézanne stayed in Aix, L'Estaque and Paris. Zola continued to help financially and also persuaded Cézanne to try to become reconciled with his father. By 1880, Cézanne and his family had moved out of Paris.

Cézanne wrote to Zola on 4 November 1878: "The reason for my letter is as follows. Hortense is in Paris on urgent business; I beg you to send her 100 francs, if you can manage that much. I'm in a real mess, but I expect to get out of it."

THE ALLOWANCE REINSTATED

Louis-Auguste did not understand his son and Cézanne, in turn, felt he could not be honest with his father, so the relationship deteriorated. Louis-Auguste suspected Cézanne had several mistresses and illegitimate children, and Cézanne, spending time in L'Estaque with Paul when Hortense was in Paris, feared a visit from his father. Yet by the end of 1878, his father relented and reinstated his full allowance – he even gave him an extra 400 francs.

LEAVING THE IMPRESSIONISTS

Since 1875, the Batignolles group had moved from the Café Guerbois to the quieter Café de la Nouvelle-Athènes on

Right: Medea, *1880. Even when he was developing his own personal technique, Cézanne tried to gain insights from his heroes. Here he was responding to the flowing style of Delacroix.*

POSITIVE REVIEWS

Monet admired Cézanne's work enormously. He recommended him to the art critics Roger Marx (1859–1913) and Gustave Geffroy (1855–1926), who went to see his work in Père Tanguy's shop, where his paintings were on display. After seeing the paintings, Marx and Geffroy wrote flattering reviews about Cézanne's great potential. However, this did little to redress the balance; other critics continued to deride him in newspaper articles.

the place Pigalle, and occasionally when he was in Paris Cézanne still joined them. But he felt even more at odds with their aims and beliefs than he had before, and was still smarting from

being singled out by critics at the Impressionist exhibitions as the most unfathomable and unbalanced artist of the group. He recognized that his work was not to everyone's taste, writing to

Zola: "I am working; poor results and too far removed from the general understanding." Yet his old friend Guillemet from Aix, who for some time had conformed to the acceptable academic standards of painting, was now part of the Salon jury. In the spring of 1879, Cézanne went to see Guillemet, who promised to commend any work he submitted to the Salon. Thus, when Pissarro invited him to participate in the fourth independent exhibition, he was particularly strongly against the idea, wanting to minimize the risk of abusive reviews and hoping to exhibit at the Salon. He replied to Pissarro's invitation: "I think that, amidst all the difficulties caused by my submitting to the Salon, it will be more suitable for me not to take part in the Impressionists' exhibition."

Below: The Poplars, c.1879–80. Cézanne was fascinated by a thicket of trees near Pontoise and captured them with a bold palette of greens and slanting brushstrokes.

Ultimately, however, Guillemet was only one voice, and the rest of the jury disagreed with him. Cézanne was once again rejected by the Salon.

NEW LANDSCAPES

From April 1879 to March 1880, Cézanne, Hortense and Paul settled in a district new to them all: the charming old town of Melun on the River Seine, about 50 kilometres (30 miles) to the south of Paris. He found the environs of Paris perfect for developing his personal style, as other *plein air* artists had done. He was particularly inspired by the river and by the poplars that grew strong and tall in light that was more subdued than that of Aix and L'Estaque. He painted quite contentedly there, including portraying a rare snow scene during the exceptionally cold winter. The paintings he produced in Melun use the same unifying tones that he had been developing in L'Estaque, and reveal how far his technique and approach had changed since the time in Pontoise and Auvers. But by removing himself from the Impressionists' circle, he had isolated himself and reduced his chances of selling his work.

Below: Self-portrait, c.1879–85. Cézanne never flattered himself in his self-portraits, but focused on the application of surface marks and colour.

Left: Rocks at L'Estaque, c.1879–82. Zola described L'Estaque: "Nothing equals the wild majesty of these gorges hollowed out between the hills… arid slopes covered with pines."

MATURING STYLE

The paintings of the late 1870s and early 1880s seem more assured than many of Cézanne's earlier works. Although they still retain the coloured shadows he had developed during his Impressionist period, he was at last establishing his mature style.

Cézanne believed that being true to nature did not necessarily mean reproducing exactly what he saw in front of him. By rearranging elements he could investigate aspects of the scene and create a certain effect.

EXACTING STANDARDS

Cézanne began to paint dynamic, harmonious compositions using muted half-tones, vivid accents and dense layers of colour. He focused on exploring the underlying structures of objects, creating colour harmonies and balanced networks of lines. Through angled brushstrokes and colour juxtapositions, he was seeking to create what he called "harmony in parallel with nature". However, he found the actual act of painting extremely difficult. His hot temper was always in danger of taking over and making him ruin his carefully composed canvases, but passionate interpretations were not part of Cézanne's intention. Instead, he wanted to examine the world and to express it in a fresh, analytical way. To this end, he painted slowly, applying every mark deliberately and carefully and spending a huge amount of time just looking at the scene in front of him, appraising the light, tones, colours, shapes and atmosphere. He tended to lose his temper with anyone who interrupted him, as he found it very difficult to re-engage with the work once his concentration was broken. If he lost his focus, he became extremely angry and often destroyed

Below: The Pool at the Jas de Bouffan, *c.1880. During the late 1880s, Cézanne painted several pictures of a road bordered with chestnut trees, and a nearby pool on the Jas de Bouffan estate.*

Above: The Artist's Wife in an Armchair, c.1881. One of 24 oil portraits of Hortense, probably painted in Paris. It portrays a harmony of colours; crimson, aubergine and turquoise.

whole canvases. He remained as critical of himself in his 40s as he had been in his 20s, when he destroyed his portraits of Zola because they did not meet his exacting standards.

THE FIFTH EXHIBITION

After his year at Melun, Cézanne moved to the outskirts of Paris, to the district known as Plaisance. He and his family lived for a year near to the lodgings he had occupied three years earlier. From there, he visited the fifth

Above: Woodland with Boulders, 1893. During the 1880s, Cézanne developed his style, forming a unique three-dimensional representation without using traditional perspective.

Impressionist exhibition, which opened on 1 April 1880 and lasted a month. Of the original group, only Degas, Pissarro, Morisot, Guillaumin and Caillebotte exhibited, joined by some new artists, including Paul Gauguin (1848–1903). The location of the exhibition was

Above: Portrait of the Artist's Son, 1881–2. In an affectionate portrait of his nine-year-old son, Cézanne has used fairly thin paint and small brushes to create a fluid and delicate image.

unfortunate as the building was being reconstructed. Attendance was poor and critics still wrote unflattering reviews.

ZOLA THE CRITIC

In May of that year, Monet and Renoir, who had abandoned the Impressionist exhibition in favour of a return to the Salon, asked Cézanne to enlist Zola's help in publicizing the bad hanging of paintings at the Salon. They wrote a letter to the Minister of Fine Arts and Cézanne sent Zola a copy. In the newspaper Le Voltaire, Zola did not merely print the letter, but commented on it in four long articles. He criticized the stuffiness of the Salon but he also wrote disparagingly about the Impressionists, declaring that "not one painter in this group has applied the new formula powerfully and definitely… we look vainly for the masterpiece which will set the seal on the formula… they remain unequal to their self-ordained task, they stammer, unable to find the right word". The Impressionists were stunned at these stinging criticisms from a former supporter. While he had triumphed, Zola clearly felt that they had failed. Cézanne had, he wrote, "the temperament of a great painter, but is still wrestling with technical difficulties".

MÉDAN, PONTOISE, AUVERS, AIX

Cézanne and Zola's friendship, while still strong, was growing more difficult since Zola had become rich and famous. Meanwhile, Cézanne was still struggling to sell paintings and trying to live on the allowance from his father.

Cézanne often received invitations to visit Zola at his home in Médan where, despite his eccentric ways, he was always greeted warmly by Zola and his wife. Several of his paintings were hanging in Zola's hall, and if he was feeling sociable, he enjoyed the company.

COMPARISONS BETWEEN FRIENDS

Since Zola's enormous success, the relationship between the two friends had been changing and the contrasts between them became marked. Zola had married his wife Gabrielle-Alexandrine in 1870, while Cézanne had not married the mother of his son. Zola was considered one of the greatest men in his field, while Cézanne was ridiculed by art critics. Zola lived the life of a wealthy and celebrated man of independent means, while Cézanne struggled to survive on his father's allowance. Underlying all this was the fact that Zola now believed Cézanne had lost his way artistically. Zola had thought that Cézanne's unpredictable behaviour and volatile moods would have calmed as he matured, but it had become clear that he would never overcome these failings, which Zola believed would always inhibit his progress. Cézanne was aware of his friend's opinions, and although he was saddened by them, remained respectful of his judgement and they retained their old affection for each other. They still wrote to each other and met often, but a rift was growing.

GAUGUIN

After Cézanne's latest rejection from the Salon and Pissarro's involvement with the sixth Impressionist exhibition from May 1881, once again Cézanne took Hortense and Paul to stay with Pissarro in Pontoise. There they were joined by Gauguin, whom Pissarro was advising on his first attempts at painting.

Above: Mill at the Couleuvre near Pontoise, c.1881. *Rows and layers of small coloured brush marks are built up in this painting. Cézanne was still influenced by Pissarro's style and approach.*

The three had long discussions and went on painting expeditions together. Gauguin had enormous admiration for Cézanne and after he had returned to his banking business in Paris, he bought five of Cézanne's paintings from Tanguy. He wrote to Pissarro: "Has Monsieur Cézanne found the exact formula for a work acceptable to everyone? If he discovers the prescription for compressing the intense expression of all his sensations into a single and unique procedure, try to make him talk in his sleep by giving him one of those mysterious homeopathic drugs and come immediately to Paris to share it with us!" This innocent and flattering remark was quoted by Pissarro to Cézanne, possibly to boost his confidence, but it aroused Cézanne's suspicions. Years later, he accused Gauguin of trying to steal what he called his 'little sensation'. Monet once declared: "Never mention Gauguin to Cézanne!"

CÉZANNE'S PALETTE

To create his precise tones and colour values, Cézanne frequently used a fairly simple palette, building up colours by careful blending, exploiting the effects of warm and cool contrasts and complementary juxtapositions. His palette of the time usually comprised lead white, zinc white, black, chrome yellow, yellow ochre, red earth or vermilion, cobalt blue, ultramarine, viridian and emerald. Occasionally he added Naples yellow, Prussian blue and chrome green. A limited palette worked well because it allowed him to harmonize subtle modulations and repeat colours across the canvas.

Cézanne still respected Pissarro's advice, but he had replaced the ethereal, fragmented Impressionist style with a more deliberate technique. Working closely from nature, he painted around Pontoise and Auvers, no longer featuring the atmospheric perspective and rarely including figures or references to Romanticism. Instead, he layered small brush marks in multiple nuances of colour.

RETURN TO PROVENCE

In mid-October 1881, Hortense and Paul returned to Paris and Cézanne went to the Jas de Bouffan, painting all day and writing to Zola and Pissarro. The peace and solitude in Provence enabled him to concentrate on his work.

Below: Leda and the Swan, *1881. Hortense was once again Cézanne's model for this voluptuous figure in one of his last paintings on classical themes.*

Below: Nude Seated on a Bank, *c.1881–4. Cézanne painted many groups of nude bathers, but occasionally he focused on a single figure, building patterns with shapes and colours.*

Above: Farmyard in Auvers, *c.1880. In the 1880s, Cézanne's light, airy tones began to give way to more marked considerations of relationships between architecture and nature.*

PORTRAITS AND THE SALON

During his career, Cézanne created a number of portraits. These were often of Hortense, but he also painted his son and numerous friends and acquaintances, and he painted over 30 self-portraits.

Cézanne worked so slowly and painstakingly, needing so many sittings for each painting, that it is no wonder his models always look tired or even annoyed. For Cézanne, this kind of work was a long, careful, sometimes frustrating process.

ANALYSIS OF STRUCTURE

Whether he was painting a landscape, a still life or a portrait, Cézanne treated all his subjects in the same way. Everything had an inner structure, which he described with colour and directional brush marks, and he modelled every object in layered tonal contrasts in order to reveal that structure. None of his portraits were created to flatter the subject and each one took a long time. Cézanne sat studying and analysing facial planes and contours, shadows and highlights, and what he called his

Below: Madame Cézanne Leaning on a Table, 1873–7. Hortense was Cézanne's most patient model. Here she looks soft and young (she was in her early 20s) and Cézanne has painted her in an Impressionistic style.

'minute sensation', which he could only obtain after hours of observation. Concentrating on physical qualities rather than personality or expression, he paid great attention to surface marks and colours. People he painted often related tales about his intense concentration when working and his despair if he could not find the correct mark. Art dealer Ambroise Vollard (1866–1939) sat for his portrait for approximately 117 sessions, each lasting two or three hours. He said: "It is difficult to imagine the extent to which on certain days his work was slow and tiresome." Gustave Geffroy endured 80 sittings, all for an unfinished painting. As was usual with all Cézanne's work, it is not entirely clear when each painting

Below: Self-portrait, 1878–80. Cézanne was usually very self-critical, but this painting shows him looking sensitive and gentle, although older than his 40 years.

Above: Madame Cézanne in the Conservatory, 1891–2. *Cézanne painted 24 mainly three-quarter-length portraits of Hortense. This unfinished painting is elegant and graceful.*

was executed as he rarely dated his canvases, but in portraits, evidence of aging is a good indicator.

PAINTING WITH RENOIR
Early in 1882, Cézanne travelled to L'Estaque. In February, Renoir went there too and stayed at a local hotel, intending to paint with Cézanne, who had fascinated him ever since Chocquet had taken such an interest in him. The two men were not close friends, but they respected each other and both were intent on showing at the Salon (Renoir had already exhibited there). Renoir loved the landscape of L'Estaque. He wrote to his dealer, Paul Durand-Ruel: "Cézanne and I are going to work together." But they did not work together for long; within a few weeks, Renoir had contracted pneumonia. Cézanne's mother travelled

Above: Self-portrait, 1879–82. *With small patches of overlapping colour, Cézanne depicts himself wearing peasant clothes and looking quite severe.*

to L'Estaque and together they nursed Renoir back to health. "I can't tell you how nice Cézanne has been to me," Renoir wrote to Chocquet the following month.

SALON ACCEPTANCE
Before Cézanne could resume his painting in L'Estaque, news came from Paris which sent him hurrying back there. After 19 fruitless years, he had been accepted at the Salon. It was not quite the good news it seemed, however, as it was the result of pressure on the selection committee by Guillemet. Over a year earlier, Zola had urged him: "Paul is still

counting on you." Cézanne's selection was only made possible by a new initiative, whereby each member of the jury could nominate one work without submitting it to the other members. But a condition was attached: the work must be painted by a pupil of the nominator. So in order to qualify, Cézanne was labelled a pupil of Guillemet, whose work he hated. His accepted painting was a portrait of his uncle that he had produced over 15 years previously. He was not elated at his success, but laughed when he thought how it would please his father.

MISPLACED OPTIMISM
Cézanne remained in Paris that summer for the first time since 1863, waiting for dealers, collectors and critics to race to his door, but none did. By September, he realized that becoming a Salon painter had not altered his fortunes, and he went to stay with Zola at Médan. In October he returned to Aix. Perhaps the best thing to emerge from his Salon acceptance was that his father had a studio built for him at the Jas de Bouffan.

SOLACE IN NATURE

On 30 April 1883, at the age of just 51, Manet died. For more than 20 years, he had been the leader of the avant-garde group of artists and writers who had originally met at the Café Guerbois.

In May, Cézanne attended Manet's funeral, together with most of the old Batignolles group. Among Manet's pall-bearers were Zola, Degas, Monet and Fantin-Latour.

CHANGING GOALS

A few days after the funeral, Cézanne returned to L'Estaque and remained there for the rest of the year. "I have rented a little house and garden at L'Estaque", he wrote to Zola. "I am still busy painting, I have some beautiful viewpoints here but they do not quite make motifs. Nevertheless, climbing the hills at sunset, one has a glorious view of Marseilles in the distance and the islands, the whole giving a most decorative effect when bathed in the evening light." He lived there in almost complete solitude. Keen to hear about all that was going on in Paris, but not to experience it first hand, he asked Zola to enliven the "long sequence of identical days" by sending him news. During the previous March (1882) the

Above: Houses of Valhermeil Seen in the Direction of Auvers-sur-Oise, *1882. With meticulous care, Cézanne applied multiple tiny brush marks, graduating each nuance and tone.*

seventh Impressionist exhibition had been held, but he did not participate. The group had lost coherence; the artists were now scattered around France, following their individual paths, which had grown out of their original collective aims. Cézanne was not the only artist to be moving into new realms. Younger artists such as Gauguin, Georges Seurat (1859–91), Vincent van Gogh (1853–90) and Henri de Toulouse-Lautrec (1864–1901) were also experimenting, inspired by Impressionism.

RENEWAL

Even though Cézanne's work was unique and inspired younger artists, in the 1880s he had not completely

Left: Mont Sainte-Victoire, c.*1882–5. By the early to mid-1880s, Cézanne had developed an extraordinary capacity to create an abundance of colour gradations.*

Above: Self-portrait, c.1880–5. With sensitive cross-hatching and firm, sure contours, Cézanne has depicted himself looking older and sterner than he was.

Below: View of the Bay of Marseilles with the Village of Saint-Henri, c.1883. From 1882–3, Cézanne painted at L'Estaque, focusing on contrasts of shapes and colours.

broken with many of the main points of Impressionism. He continued to explore the multiple colours of objects, created by light, reflections, shadows and scientific phenomena. By the 1880s, he had eliminated emotion from his work and was aiming to express permanence, as opposed to the Impressionists, who conveyed transience. His compositions were carefully constructed objective views of places he enjoyed or recalled from his childhood, or studies of still lifes or bathers. During this period, he painted the same subjects over and over again.

FAMILY DIFFICULTIES

Cézanne's relationship with Hortense was unusual. They spent more time apart than together, and although they had an 11-year-old son, and Cézanne's father now knew about him, they had not married. His work was still not respected by any but a few avant-garde artists, and his father treated him with condescension. His mother and sister Marie doted on him, but they did not understand his art or his morals and urged him to sort out his affairs with Hortense. Although he had friends, he did not mix readily and he often felt excluded, which led him to shun company and choose to spend his time alone.

LANDSCAPE PAINTING

Landscapes appeared as important backgrounds in early Renaissance paintings and became a valid genre across Europe during the early 16th century. They did not become a respected separate form of painting until a few centuries later. Even Rubens, who loved painting landscapes, could not concentrate on them until he was a successful court painter and had gone into semi-retirement. When Cézanne began his landscapes, the Barbizon painters and the Impressionists had paved the way for him to search for truths about the structure of the natural world.

ACUTE OBSERVATIONS

As ever, Cézanne did not want to follow fashion or to paint as other artists did. Instead, he sought to capture what was enduring in his subject, to discover and portray something that might not be apparent to other observers.

Cézanne's aim was to paint something that had not been painted before, in his own style. He began depicting objects from more than one perspective at once, trying to convey a sense of permanence.

CAREFUL OBSERVATION

The formula for each painting remained necessarily (for Cézanne) controlled and calculated. Before he even put a mark on the canvas, he would spend a long time observing the subject, trying to understand its essence, character or atmosphere. Next, still closely focusing on the subject, he would mark out the structure – this was like an underlying framework that underpinned all forms. Finally, deliberately and carefully, he

Below: Madame Cézanne, c.1883–5. *Cézanne's portrayals of Hortense are detached, as if he viewed her in the same way as his still lifes, contemplating only how forms and tones relate to each other and how planes interlock.*

POST-IMPRESSIONISM

It is understandable that Cézanne has often been linked with the Impressionists, but he has also been associated with the Post-Impressionists. Like many artists, he is difficult to categorize but seems to have been influenced by both movements. The two groups of artists explored similar elements such as light and colour; many of them were friends, and discussed and developed their ideas together. Whereas the Impressionists focused on light, the transience of nature and blurring details, the Post-Impressionists concentrated on colour, often flattening forms and creating new visual theories with their art. Post-Impressionism, even more than Impressionism, is an umbrella term for a wide range of styles, and Cézanne and Seurat represented two different aspects of the new trend. Both artists showed evidence of Impressionist influence in their use of colour, but whereas Cézanne applied colour thickly, using short, quite choppy brushstrokes, Seurat placed dots of primary colours adjacent to each other on his canvases, so that in the viewers' eyes they would appear to blend. This is a technique that is known as Divisionism or Pointillism, and it developed directly from Chevreul's theory that complementary colours, such as blue and orange, become more vivid when juxtaposed. Gauguin and Van Gogh are also classed as Post-Impressionists. Their aim was to capture light and colour, but they also portrayed emotional expression and symbolism.

Above: Viaduct at L'Estaque, c.1883. *This light-filled view is built up of Cézanne's diagonal brushstrokes, with balanced colours and straight and curved lines.*

Right: Bay of L'Estaque, c.1879–83. *Emphasizing colour changes with many tiny brush marks, Cézanne has focused on clouds and water, two elements he rarely painted elsewhere.*

began building up the forms, colours, textures and tones, describing them with pertinently angled marks. These forms, colours, textures and tones were not necessarily what anyone else might have seen, but to him they were the most important elements – the essence of the subject. He often included more colours and structures than the eye could perceive from one viewpoint, so he could show the whole object, not just one aspect of it. This is why most of his paintings are not photographically realistic. He was not aiming for that sort of image, but attempting to grasp underlying structures and to illustrate them on two-dimensional surfaces. He had no desire to recreate the world as a photographer could now do, or as artists had tried to do for centuries. He saw that as superficial imitation, and invalid for artists to attempt now that photography had been invented. He deconstructed and then re-formed what he saw, projecting his personal interpretations of the world on to the canvas in a revolutionary way.

REPEATED MOTIFS

For several years, Cézanne returned to Marseilles almost as frequently as he returned to Aix. He continued painting

many views of L'Estaque, especially its roofs, factories, pine trees and rocky slopes, always including an expanse of sea and sky. The irregular shapes of the trees and little cubes of houses nestling together made a unique theme, with vibrant colours that were intensified by the bright sunlight. Despite being an artist who tried not to paint in dramatic

Above: L'Estaque, View of the Gulf of Marseilles, 1878–9. *With fairly even tonal contrasts, this painting creates an impression of depth without the use of atmospheric perspective.*

light effects, he wrote to Zola: "Long live the sun, which gives us such beautiful light."

PAINTING WITH FRIENDS

Renoir had thoroughly enjoyed painting with Cézanne in L'Estaque during the previous year, and he had been touched by the kindness the gruff artist had shown him when he had contracted pneumonia and required nursing.

Monet and Renoir were both fascinated by Cézanne's work, and in December 1883, they visited him on their way back from a tour of the Mediterranean coast. They understood and respected his single-mindedness and originality as they were pursuing similar paths.

SOLIDITY AND STRUCTURE

Cézanne continued to paint in his unique manner, using many of the influences he had picked up during his career, such as Pissarro's short brushstrokes, the rough realities of Courbet and the open-air painting of Corot and Monet. He even referred back to Baroque painting and other traditional styles. It was this monumentality that he was trying to attain, something more solid – he felt – than the Impressionists' transient, momentary effects of light. He sat with tenacious resolve in front of his subjects, contemplating the inner substance or matter from which they were constructed. So the placement of objects was important, and all his compositions, whether still lifes, figures or landscapes, were arranged and worked out carefully. He built up every surface with variegated brush marks, applied at different angles and in different directions, to describe everything before him most expressively.

PERSPECTIVE THROUGH COLOUR

By this time, Monet's and Renoir's work was becoming popular (in 1883, they each had successful one-man exhibitions in Paris), while recognition still seemed to elude Cézanne. Unlike most critics and collectors, the two Impressionists understood and respected Cézanne's non-traditional approach to depicting space and structure through colour and mark, within balanced compositions, using a wide variety of colours mixed from

Above: Vase of Flowers, *c.1889, Renoir. Renoir's modelling of forms through small brush marks of colour became visibly more definite after working with Cézanne.*

a reduced palette. Judicious application of cool and warm colours across the canvas rather than strong tonal contrasts was one of the ways that

Right: Landscape with a Red Roof, *1875–6. The dark trunk of the pine tree compels viewers to peer around it to the intricate landscape beyond.*

he achieved his aims. "I try to render perspective through colour alone," he explained. "I proceed very slowly, for nature reveals herself to me in very complex form and constant progress must be made."

TWO-DIMENSIONAL PAINTINGS

Since the 15th century, traditional Western painting had featured converging lines and vanishing points to convey the effects of perspective. Cézanne believed this method was artificial and irrelevant. Because he did not adhere to these traditional methods of linear perspective, he could paint objects in any size he chose. While he did not play with dimensions quite as overtly as the ancient Egyptians, he frequently matched an object's size to the importance he felt it should have within the composition.

The intended result was to make viewers aware that they were looking at two-dimensional canvases and not to give them the illusion of reality.

REPEATED VIEWS

He had focused on a fairly narrow range of subjects for several years. In the early 1880s, he began painting even fewer themes. These were not the same views depicted in different lights, as Monet explored, but paintings that recorded the same or similar views and objects, sometimes from slightly different viewpoints, each showing different ways of creating a new reality.

Below: Portrait of Cézanne, Renoir, *1880. Unlike Cézanne's self-portraits, this pastel by Renoir shows the sensitive side of Cézanne's nature, which Renoir had experienced at first hand.*

Above: The Blue Vase, c.1889–90. By bathing this in frontal light and using unexpected colours, Cézanne created a particularly original and atypical still life.

JORIS-KARL HUYSMANS

The novelist J.-K. Huysmans (1848–1907) was one of the few visitors to Zola's house at Médan whom Cézanne liked. However, in 1883, Huysmans published a book, *L'Art Moderne,* in which he praised the Impressionists, but did not mention Cézanne. Pissarro wrote to him, enquiring: "Why is it that you do not say a word about Cézanne, whom all of us recognize as one of the most astounding and curious temperaments of our time and who has had a very great influence on modern art?" Huysmans immediately replied: "I find Cézanne's personality congenial, for I know through Zola of his efforts, his vexations and his defeats when he tries to create a work! Yes, he has temperament, he is an artist, but in total, with the exception of some still lifes, the rest is, to my mind, not likely to live. It is interesting, curious, suggestive in ideas, but… in my humble opinion, the Cézannes typify the Impressionists who didn't make the grade."

BETRAYAL AND DESPAIR

In the spring of 1885, Cézanne wrote to Zola, 'Trahit sua quemque voluptas', which translates as 'Each man to his own taste'. He had fallen in love with another woman, but the affair was to be short-lived.

The woman Cézanne loved has not been identified, and how they met is not known either, but in another letter to Zola, he confessed he felt "tortured by anxiety". Apart from his brief feelings for Hortense when he met her, this was the only love affair he ever experienced and it affected him badly. Over the following months, Cézanne enlisted Zola's help in receiving letters from the woman, known only as Fanny,

so that Hortense would not find out. In June, after several months of anguish, he, Hortense and Paul went to stay with Renoir at La Roche-Guyon, not far from Monet's home in Giverny. But he could not concentrate and continued to suffer with the debilitating headaches that had started at the beginning of the year. It is not clear exactly what happened, but by August, the affair was over. Before he left La Roche-Guyon, he

wrote to Zola: "I cannot find anything here that I can use in my present state. I have decided to return to Aix as soon as possible. Before I do, I shall visit Médan to shake your hand. For myself, there is only absolute isolation…"

FRIENDSHIP'S END

Yet something even more shattering to Cézanne's equilibrium was about to occur. In March 1886, Zola's novel

Above: Dying Slave, after Michelangelo. *Cézanne made many studies of artists he esteemed, including this sensuous rendition of Michelangelo's dying slave.*

Right: Bathsheba, *1885. Cézanne painted the woman who captivated King David at the time that he himself was in the throes of a secret and passionate love affair.*

L'Oeuvre (*The Masterpiece*) was published. It was the story of an artist called Claude Lantier, who could not finish a work he had been painting for years. Eventually he committed suicide in front of his canvas, never having achieved his ultimate goals. Lantier bears a striking resemblance to Cézanne, especially as his childhood experiences closely resemble Cézanne's, of which Zola, of course, was a part. For instance, he wrote: "…when [Claude and his two friends, Pierre and Louis] were about twelve they had a passion for playing about in the deeper portions of the stream; they swam like fish… they practically lived in the river." Later Zola described Lantier's lack of confidence: "…he began to slip back into his old fits of doubt… every picture rejected he pronounced bad… it was this feeling of impotence that exasperated him… What was really unbearable was the inability ever to express himself to the full…" He continued: "As his crises recurred more and more frequently, he would spend weeks in unbearable self-torture, hovering between hope and uncertainty, and through all the weary hours he spent wrestling with his rebellious masterpiece one great mainstay was the consoling dream of the picture which he would paint one day." Even Cézanne's problems with women were referred to, including his relationship with one woman, with whom he has a son. The whole novel was uncomfortably similar to Cézanne's life.

Zola's motives for writing this novel are not clear. More than most, it gives details of personal memories (in his notes, he constantly used the actual names of his friends rather than the fictitious ones in the book). It was not an outstanding work and he must have been aware of the deep wounds it would inflict on his closest friend.

CÉZANNE'S REACTION

In the end, when Zola sent Cézanne a copy soon after its publication, the novel must have seemed to Cézanne the ultimate act of betrayal. He sent a note back, simply stating: "…I have just received *L'Oeuvre* which you were kind

Above: The Village of Gardanne, 1885–6. *Cézanne balanced warm and cool colours against descriptive tones, juxtaposing the blocky forms of the town with the organic shapes of the vegetation.*

enough to send to me. I thank the author… for this kind token of remembrance and ask him to allow me to clasp his hand in memory of bygone years. Ever yours under the impulse of past times." There is no evidence of any further communication between the two men for the rest of their lives, although when Zola died in a tragic accident in September 1902, Cézanne shut himself in his studio and wept.

Right: The Bather, 1885. *This figure appears ungainly and inelegant against the bare landscape. Colours and tones are echoed across the canvas.*

A TROUBLED YEAR

The year 1886 was possibly the most stressful of Cézanne's life. He had severed his friendship with Zola at the beginning of the year, and by the end, his personal situation had irrevocably changed once more.

Cézanne had only just managed to regain his painting rhythm after his love affair ended the previous year. The break with Zola affected his work yet again.

MARRIAGE

Cézanne was traumatized, first by his unhappy love affair and then by Zola's book. Family urgings to legalize his relationship with Hortense now came to a head, with Louis-Auguste acknowledging the liaison and even giving his consent. The family had a low opinion of Hortense, but she was the mother of his child and their liaison had continued for so long that the family

believed he should legitimize his 14-year-old son. So on 28 April 1886, in the presence of his parents and other family members, the 47-year-old artist married Hortense at a civil ceremony at the Hôtel de Ville in Aix-en-Provence. His sister Rose's husband, Maxime Conil, was one of the witnesses. The next day, they had a church ceremony in the presence of Conil and Cézanne's sister Marie, plus two other witnesses.

BREAKING WITH ZOLA

Cézanne's troubled state of mind over Zola overwhelmed him. Even though all the Impressionists were also offended

Above: Still Life with Apples and Pears, c.1891–2. The fruit shown in this painting was grown locally near Aix, and like Mont Sainte-Victoire, it became symbolic of Cézanne's beloved home.

by the book and both Guillemet and Huysmans criticized it, this did not make his pain any easier to bear. Guillemet wrote to Zola: "A very gripping but a very depressing book… Everyone in it is discouraged, works badly, thinks badly. People endowed with genius or failures all end up by doing poor work… Reality is not so sad, fortunately… In your latest book I find only sadness or

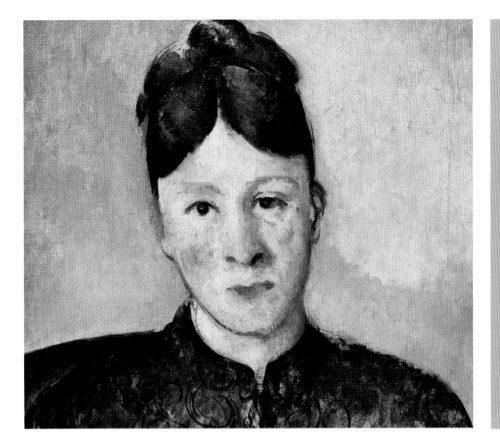

Above: Portrait of Madame Cézanne, *c.1885. Hortense sat for Cézanne often. Here, her face is an almost perfect oval and she radiates serenity and calm.*

impotence… Let us hope, by God, that the little gang, as Madame Zola calls it, does not try to recognize themselves in your uninteresting heroes, for they are evil into the bargain."

Monet also wrote to him: "… I have always enjoyed reading your books and this one was doubly interesting to me because it raises questions about art for which we have been fighting so long. I have just read it and I am worried and upset, I admit." Zola's replies are not known, but from that point on, he and the painters who were formerly his friends no longer met. Although they were all following the creative paths they had aimed for when they first set out as artists, it seems that in Zola's eyes, their work had not achieved what he had anticipated. His ideas moved on a different path, and naturally they felt hurt that he criticized them simply because he misunderstood them. Even Van Gogh, who admired the novelist, wrote to a friend: "I am not among those who are furious at him for having written that book. Through it I am learning to know Zola. I am learning to know his weak side, to realize that his knowledge of the art of painting is insufficient, that it is, in this particular case, because he has some defects."

Below: Portrait of Madame Cézanne, *1885–90. This portrait emphasizes tranquillity, simplicity and serenity with delicately subtle shades of brownish-green to sky blue.*

THE EIGHTH IMPRESSIONIST EXHIBITION

From 15 May to 15 June 1886, the eighth Impressionist exhibition was held on the second floor of a well-known restaurant, the Maison Dorée on the corner of the rue Lafitte and the boulevard des Italiens, . There were 246 works on show, but the only artists participating from the original group were Pissarro and Degas. Other contributors included Gauguin, Seurat and Paul Signac (1863–1935), who painted independently, but not in the manner of the Impressionists. Impressionism was no longer the single-minded movement it had been in 1874, but had developed in different directions.

LOUIS-AUGUSTE

Six months after the book's publication and Cézanne's marriage, on 23 October 1886, Louis-Auguste died aged 88, leaving his son as head of the family. For the first time in his life, he was wealthy and independent, with 400,000 francs a year, plus 25,000 for Hortense and Paul.

Below: Avenue at Chantilly, *1888. In 1888, Cézanne spent five months at Chantilly, north of Paris. This picture was probably painted in the park surrounding the château.*

LEAVING THE JAS DE BOUFFAN

For Hortense, marrying Cézanne did not make their relationship any closer. She and young Paul chose to spend most of their time in Paris while Cézanne remained at Aix-en-Provence, painting in his usual solitary manner.

Cézanne began withdrawing into his painting even more, while his mother and Marie continued to run the household. He had plenty of time to ponder on his recent sorrows, and felt more desolate and misunderstood than ever.

TIME FOR REFLECTION

Despite Louis-Auguste's sternness, he had been a permanent source of strength at the Jas de Bouffan and now that he was gone, Cézanne was responsible for his mother, his sister Marie and his wife and son (his younger sister, Rose was married). In hindsight, Cézanne recognized his father's good qualities, including common sense, calmness and self-assurance, and he regretted that during Louis-Auguste's lifetime he had never made his father proud. Now his mother was in her 70s, he hoped to reward her enduring faith in him by making a name for himself.

A DIFFICULT RELATIONSHIP

For the first time in his life, he had the means to do all the things that other artists did, such as travelling to Spain and Italy to see the work of artists he had always admired. However, he chose to remain in Aix. Hortense used her delicate health as an excuse to stay in Paris and avoid the place she found boring and the husband she had not loved for years. Although his mother and his sister often tried to mediate the couple's frequent rows, neither of them liked Hortense. Cézanne found her lack of intelligence irritating and she did not understand either his art or his attachment to Aix. Cézanne was shy and thoughtful, quick to lose his temper, passionate and often anguished; Hortense did not think deeply, did not care for art and she gambled. On the positive side, she was a good mother

Above: The Jas de Bouffan, 1885–7. *A view of the home Cézanne loved, painted from several different viewpoints at once to reveal more than an outward appearance.*

to their son and Cézanne's most patient model, repeatedly sitting for him without moving for hours.

PUBLIC BETRAYAL

Cézanne's thoughts also persistently slid back to his break with Zola and his motives for writing such a book. It was certain that the character Claude Lantier represented Cézanne, since in Zola's notes for the book, he often wrote 'Paul' instead of 'Claude'. Although Cézanne had been aware that their relationship had been changing for some time and that Zola's belief in his artistic promise had waned, the book was still a shock. Cézanne's own doubts about his progress often surfaced, but

Above: The Aqueduct (Mont Sainte-Victoire Seen through Trees), *c.1885–7. The aqueduct in the Arc valley appears in many of Cézanne's paintings. This time it is painted from Rose and Maxime's house.*

underneath it all, he believed in his ability to create art that was revolutionary and unique. Zola's public declaration that Cézanne was a failure was subjective, unprovoked and cruel and their broken friendship, after 34 years, left a gaping hole in his life.

NO PLACE LIKE HOME

Amid all this emotional turmoil, the main constants in Cézanne's life were his painting, his mother, his sister Marie, his son Paul and the Jas de Bouffan. Since his father had built him the studio under the roof at the Jas de Bouffan, he had used it often, although he still spent much of his time painting *en plein air*. After the death of his father, he moved his studio to a large room on the ground floor, where he could bring canvases back from outside and carry on working. The paintings he created at the Jas de Bouffan were variations on subjects he had been working on for years, including the grounds and buildings and the countryside, but he never tired of them. Their familiarity

Below: Trees in a Park at the Jas de Bouffan, *1885–7. Cézanne described both the light breeze in the autumn air and the solidity of the trees and buildings. Here he managed to capture his 'little sensation'.*

Above: The Alley of Chestnut Trees at the Jas de Bouffan, c.*1888. Cézanne has portrayed the beauty of the grounds of the Jas de Bouffan, balancing colour in a patchwork of brush marks on the canvas.*

meant that he could concentrate on other aspects beyond superficial appearances. He still returned to Paris periodically, but spent most of his time in Aix. When his mother died in October 1897, the estate was split three ways between himself and his sisters. His brother-in-law, Maxime Conil, Rose's husband, insisted on selling the property in order to receive his share of the money. On 18 September 1899, the Jas de Bouffan, his beloved family home for 40 years, was sold, and the proceeds were divided between the three siblings.

MONT SAINTE-VICTOIRE

The imposing mountain Mont Sainte-Victoire dominates the landscape of Aix, rising majestically above the surrounding hills, vineyards and rivers. Cézanne was fascinated by the Mont Sainte-Victoire all his life, and painted it over and over again.

Cézanne described the mountain as a 'stunning subject'. In his paintings of it he aimed to depict its solidity and permanence through coloured patches, usually without reference to linear or atmospheric perspective.

A CONSTANT MOTIF

During the last 15 years of his life, Cézanne painted the Mont Sainte-Victoire nearly 60 times, from differing viewpoints and in diverse lights and weather conditions. Situated 10 kilometres (6 miles) east of Aix, the mountain could be seen clearly from his sister and brother-in-law's farm at Bellevue, and this was his main vantage point for painting it during the 1880s. Bellevue was on a hill with a fine view across the valley of the river Arc (where Cézanne and Zola played as children). Another favourite location was a hill between Bellevue and Montbriant, the neighbouring farm. The panoramic views afforded from these spots included the valley, the railway, a viaduct and pine trees. The land that stretched out before him to the base of the mountain was filled with the deep greens, oranges and browns of pine woods, while the rocky limestone mountain reflected soft blues, greys, pinks and oranges from the sky and adjacent land. According to legend, the red earth of the adjacent plain acquired its colour from the blood of invading Teutons who were beaten in battle by the Romans in 102BC.

The Mont Sainte-Victoire was an ideal motif for him: it not only came to symbolize his quest to paint something solid and enduring, but was also a way

Below: Mont Sainte-Victoire, *1885–7. In one of his most dramatic views, Cézanne has framed the painting with the trunk and branch of a pine, which echoes the contour of the mountain.*

Above: Mont Sainte-Victoire. The mountain dominates Aix-en-Provence and could be seen by Cézanne from most of his favourite locations.

Above left: Mont Sainte-Victoire, Renoir, 1889. In Aix, Renoir painted Cézanne's favourite motif in an Impressionist style.

Above: The Kintai Bridge in Suho, Hokusai, c.1831. This simple composition showing the sacred Mount Fuji can be directly compared to Cézanne's paintings of Mont Sainte-Victoire.

of pulling himself out of the depression that threatened to overwhelm him. Inspired by the magnificence of the mountain, he painted it with a relentless intensity that few artists have devoted to any subject.

INTENSE OBSERVATION

The paintings were his homage to his home and attest to his love of nature as well as his development as an artist. No matter how many times he painted it, he first spent a great deal of time observing and identifying each element's internal structure (as with all his other works) before he set about painting. Over time, these sustained studies of nature became flatter, more fragmented and even less realistic. By distilling the forms he observed to geometric shapes and creating spatial harmonies through colour, he heralded the major pictorial movements of the 20th century. As he said: "You have to reflect. The eye is not enough, reflection is vital."

CLASSICAL PERIOD

Cézanne's paintings of the 1880s later became known as his 'classical period'. The term arose from his exploitation of Nicolas Poussin's (1594–1665) ideas about painting an ideal, ordered world – balancing objective and subjective elements in structured compositions. Poussin organized his landscapes carefully, focusing on what he himself

saw as well as what he wanted viewers to see, and Cézanne did so too. He said he intended "to redo Poussin over again according to nature". He did not hide the fact that he was trying to create something monumental and impressive, as Poussin had done, making original and unique art out of the earlier artist's ideas and practices.

EXHIBITIONS

Despite his overpowering feelings of anguish and depression over recent events, Cézanne still wanted the public to recognize his work. However, he did not want to risk having further scathing reviews written about him.

In 1888, Cézanne spent more time in Paris, staying in the studio he had occupied next to Guillaumin in 1875, the same room that Zola had described as Claude Lantier's studio. While he was there, he saw only Guillaumin and occasionally Chocquet, who remained his most ardent fan.

FAVOURABLE REVIEWS

Cézanne did not stay long in the studio, however, but spent five months painting in the outskirts of Paris, mainly around Chantilly and in the Fontainebleau forest. That year, for the first time, some events occurred that indicated that he was beginning to be regarded in a more positive light. After criticizing him in the past, that year Huysmans published an article describing him favourably. This might have been simply Huysmans' way of redressing the balance after the publication of Zola's novel, but it could also have been a genuine reappraisal of Cézanne's work. He referred to Cézanne as "a much ignored painter" and the following year, in his book *Certains* (1889), he devoted an entire chapter to Cézanne, describing him as "a colourist of revealing powers, who contributed more than Manet to the Impressionist movement".

THE EXPOSITION UNIVERSELLE

In 1887, construction of the Eiffel Tower began in Paris in preparation for the 1889 Exposition Universelle, a World's Fair that would mark the centennial celebration of the French Revolution. The Eiffel Tower was to be the entrance arch to the fair, but it met with huge criticism from the public. Contemporary newspapers were filled with angry letters from the official art community, calling it an eyesore and 'an odious column built up of riveted iron plates'.

Above: Chestnut Trees at the Jas de Bouffan, c.1885–7. *Cézanne rearranged the chestnut trees in his composition to create an almost symmetrical arrangement of intertwined branches, with Mont Sainte-Victoire in the background.*

On Chocquet's insistence, Cézanne agreed that his painting, *The House of the Hanged Man*, should be exhibited in the Centennial Exhibition of French Art at the World's Fair. The works of Manet, Monet and Pissarro were also exhibited there. It was the first time (apart from the Salon exhibition in 1882) that Cézanne had exhibited his work since 1877.

LES VINGT

At the end of 1889, the Brussels lawyer, publisher and entrepreneur Octave Maus (1856–1919) invited Cézanne to show at an annual Brussels exhibition with the Belgian group called 'Les XX' (Les Vingt, or The Twenty). This was a group of 20 Belgian painters, designers

THE SOCIETY OF INDEPENDENT ARTISTS

Largely due to the reverberations the Impressionists had generated, a Society of Independent Artists was formed in Paris in the summer of 1884, founded among others by Seurat, Signac and Odilon Redon (1840–1916). Their motto was 'No jury or awards' and they claimed: "... the purpose of the Société des Artistes Indépendants – based on the principle of abolishing admission jury – is to allow the artists to present their works to public judgement with complete freedom". At their first exhibition, the centre of attention was Seurat's *Bathing at Asnières* (1883–4), which embodied scientific colour theories. The Society's exhibitions brought new artistic notions to the fore.

Right: The Central Dome of the Universal Exhibition of 1889, *Louis Beroud, 1889–90. The Fourth World Exposition celebrated the centenary of the French Revolution and was held in Paris from May to October 1889, attracting 28 million visitors.*

and sculptors with distinct Impressionist and Post-Impressionist inclinations that Maus had formed in 1883. Each year, 20 international artists were also invited to participate. The exhibitions were intended for the whole European avant-garde and were set up to bring new ideas in art to a wider public. Over the years, the international artists involved included Pissarro, Monet, Seurat, Gauguin and Van Gogh. Cézanne was reluctant at first, still wary of the cutting criticism he might attract. However, Maus was persuasive and Cézanne wrote to him, agreeing to submit three works: "In view of the pleasure of finding myself in such good company, I do not hesitate to modify my resolve." Hanging alongside his canvases at the exhibition were works by Sisley and Van Gogh.

Below: Postcard of the Paris Universal Exhibition of 1889. The 1889 fair was held on the Champ de Mars and its main symbol was the Eiffel Tower, designed by Gustave Eiffel.

Above: Avenue at Chantilly, 1888. *Painted at the same time as* Avenue at Chantilly *on page 75, cool blues and greens are balanced by warm tones.*

PAINTING IN WATERCOLOUR

Cézanne painted in watercolour throughout his career, but his method of using the medium changed considerably after 1880, when it became a more important means for him to explore structure, space and colour and also influenced the way he used oils.

Watercolour was a way for Cézanne to explore his themes and capture colours and sensations. By the end of his life, he was producing his largest, most complex and colourful watercolours.

JEWEL COLOURS
Because he was still intent on capturing the inner structure of things, the way Cézanne used the medium challenged conventions, as did his whole approach to art. He worked in graphite pencil first and then applied the watercolour in a smooth, flowing manner, using not only the colour, but also the white of the underlying paper to create a sense of order and harmony while conveying the substance of his subjects. In accordance with the Impressionists' approach, he identified local and reflected colours as he painted, picking up bright contrasts or unusually coloured highlights and shadows. He used the transparency of watercolour to create brilliant combinations and juxtapositions. It enabled him to work more speedily, although every stage was still carefully considered.

Although Cézanne's watercolours seem unfinished at a first glance, each contains the essential components of a complete composition. They seem spontaneous rather than overworked, but in fact they involved a complex building-up of layers of washes.

NEW TECHNIQUE
From about 1885, he began producing watercolours with even more zest, working out his creative problems through the translucency of the medium, using bold and vibrant colours. By the late 1890s he had developed the ability to capture exceptionally finely nuanced effects, applying kaleidoscopic colours and leaving the white of the paper exposed in places to create colourful depths and bright accents.

Above: Study of Trees, *c.1890. Firm pencil marks and resonant watercolour washes depict the rhythms of these elegant branches and leaves.*

He always used light graphite pencil lines to create basic structures and applied jewelled hues in transparent layers over these, flooding in colour where extra definition was needed and ultimately creating the impression of dynamism and immediacy.

AN INTIMATE STYLE
Although oil paints were his favourite medium, Cézanne's watercolours reveal clues about his working methods with both types of paint: what he looked for initially, what he wanted to emphasize,

Left: Still Life with Apples, Bottle and Chairback, *1904–6. This shows Cézanne's technique of drawing in pencil first, then adding transparent washes of modulated colour. The bright hues are accented by the whiteness of the paper showing through.*

and the importance of colour. His watercolours were never intended for public exhibition, as they were nearly always meant to be precursory sketches for his main works. They were often more personal and intimate than his oils. It was in his watercolours that he devised the 'colour patch' system, whereby he applied small patches of different colours to build an image. These became an important element of his later oil paintings. Toward the end of the 1880s, he created tapestry-like networks of oil-paint patches in variations of colour that resembled his watercolours, indicating how he created his 'little sensations'. Gradation and modulating colours were each paramount to his approach in both watercolour and oils. "I never wanted and I shall never accept a lack of modelling or gradation," he said, and "There is no such thing as line and modelling, there are only contrasts."

SWITZERLAND

In the summer of 1890, Cézanne made his first trip abroad, travelling to Switzerland with Hortense and Paul. Hortense had some questions of inheritance that she needed to sort out, and they spent five months in Switzerland. Cézanne was beginning to feel the ill-effects of the onset of diabetes, which made him particularly irritable.

Above: The Garden Terrace at Les Lauves, 1902–6. Cézanne painted this view from the studio he built in Les Lauves, in the north of Aix. The painting was originally owned by the collector Ambroise Vollard.

On their return from Switzerland in November, Cézanne went back to Aix and Hortense and Paul returned to Paris. But by the following February, Cézanne reduced the allowance he was sending Hortense, so that she was forced to leave Paris and return to Aix to live with their son.

Since Hortense had fallen out with Cézanne's mother and sisters, she was not a welcome visitor at the Jas de Bouffan, and Cézanne preferred to be alone, so his solution to the problem was to rent them an apartment in Aix while he stayed at the family home.

Left: Still Life with Green Melon, 1902–6. Cézanne laid down rich layers of pigment to create the illusion of depth and shadow. Light is evoked through the paint's transparency.

GAINING FAME

By the early 1890s, there was a distinct contrast between those in the art world who supported and admired Cézanne and treated him with a new respect, and those who continued to deride him.

In Paris, Cézanne was attracting positive attention from several avant-garde artists and critics, while the official art establishment and Zola's circle condescendingly continued to denigrate his work.

PÈRE TANGUY'S SHOP
Gradually, word spread that Cézanne's work could be viewed at Père Tanguy's dark little shop. Curious artists, including Van Gogh, Signac, Seurat, Émile Bernard (1868–1941) and Maurice Denis (1870–1943), plus collectors such as Vollard, began meeting there, marvelling at the originality of the paintings and how Cézanne reduced nature to pictorial elements, eliminating all others. Bernard recalled: "One went there as to a museum to see the few sketches by the unknown artist who lived in Aix, dissatisfied with his work and with the world, who himself destroyed these studies, objects of admiration though they were. The magnificent qualities of this true painter appeared even more original because of their author's

legendary character. Members of the Institute, influential and avant-garde critics visited the modest shop in the rue Clauzel, which thus became the fable of Paris and the conversation of the studios. Nothing seemed more

Above: Bathers in front of a Tent, *c.1883–7. None of Cézanne's figures face out of his canvases. Instead, all remain anonymous, distorted in shape and linked to each other through structure and colour.*

disconcerting than these canvases, where the most outstanding gifts were coupled with a childlike naivety; the young felt the genius, the old the folly of the paradox; the jealous saw only impotence."

Even those who visited but did not admire Cézanne's paintings were touched by Tanguy's obvious estimation of them. An American critic, who had been taken to see the paintings in 1892, recounted: "[Tanguy] has a curious way of first looking down at his picture with all the fond love of a mother and then

Left: Male Bathers, *c.1890. Focusing on the bodies as powerful structures and turning them into near-abstractions, Cézanne set his bathers in an unreal, personally created world.*

AMBROISE VOLLARD

In 1887, Vollard arrived in Paris as a law student, having been born and raised in Réunion, an overseas colony of France in the Indian Ocean. Between lectures he wandered the banks of the Seine, hunting the bookstalls for prints and drawings and laying the foundations of his career as one of the most astute art dealers of his generation. Rather than taking up a career in law, he worked as a clerk for an art dealer and, in 1893, he opened his own art gallery on rue Lafitte. He was one of the first dealers not only to recognize Cézanne's potential, but to act on his judgement.

Above: Study of Bathers, c.1895–8. *Aiming to achieve a complete fusion of the human figure and the landscape, Cézanne reproduced figures from other works and even from magazines.*

looking up at you over his glasses, as if begging you to admire his beloved children… I could not help feeling, apart from all opinions of my own, that a movement in art that can inspire such devotion must have a deeper final import than the mere ravings of a coterie."

MONUMENTAL FIGURES

Throughout his life, Cézanne drew figures in his sketchbooks, frequently copying classical sculptures (he went to the Louvre every morning when he was in Paris) or practising what he had learned during his brief academic studies. Copying the masters was one of the most important aspects of his training, and figures in landscapes were one of the subjects he was most attracted to, particularly in the work of artists such as Giorgione, Titian, Rubens and Poussin. The main aim of these artists was to depict beauty while relating mythological or religious stories. In contrast, Cézanne focused on colour and structure, concentrating on creating harmony between the figures and the

landscape. His figures appear distorted because he was not trying to portray perfect human forms. In a letter to his son he said his primary goal was to "create as rich a harmony as possible" and a "harmonious unity between man and nature". His bathers are always surrounded by the intensified colours of nature, predominantly greens and blues. By depicting only male or female figures in each work, he

Above: Bathers in the Open Air, *c.1890–1. Cézanne's bathers were an open challenge to the academic nudes of the Salon, and were inspired by memories of his childhood sojourns with Zola.*

eliminated any implications of sexual involvement of the characters, making the composition the focal aspect; by not focusing on beauty, he aimed to imbue his work with a timeless quality.

SALES AND RECOGNITION

The late 1880s and early 1890s were years of even greater self-doubt for Cézanne. He quarrelled with almost everyone who visited him at Aix, including Renoir and an old friend from the Académie Suisse, Francisco Oller (1833–1917).

Cézanne's mood swings were becoming worse, exacerbated by his diabetes. Friends naturally became wary of visiting him. Then his greatest promoters, Chocquet and Tanguy, died.

IRRITABILITY AND FRIENDSHIP

In late 1889, Renoir stayed in Aix with his wife and son, renting Bellevue for a few months from Maxime Conil and often painting with Cézanne in the Arc valley. Considering how close the two artists had become over recent years, this seemed the perfect consolation for Cézanne's sorrow over the Zola affair. However, after a short stay at

Above: Père Tanguy, Van Gogh, 1887–8. *Behind Tanguy, Van Gogh has painted numerous Japanese prints of the kind that many artists collected. Tanguy sits like a revered icon in the centre of the work.*

THE LEGACY OF CAILLEBOTTE

Caillebotte's family inheritance enabled him to help fund Impressionist exhibitions and to support his fellow artists by buying their works when they were short of money. After his untimely death, despite his provision that his collection should remain undivided and ultimately be displayed in the Louvre, officials would not accept the paintings. In 1896, the French State authorized the National Museums to select some paintings from the embarrassing Caillebotte legacy to be exhibited in the Musée du Luxembourg. Académie officials refused 27 paintings out of the 67 in the collection, which was humiliating for the artists concerned. The accepted works were: seven pastels by Degas; two out of four works by Manet; eight out of sixteen paintings by Monet; six out of eight works by Renoir; seven out of eighteen by Pissarro; and two out of five works by Cézanne.

---

the Jas de Bouffan, Renoir left, later complaining to Monet: "We had to suddenly leave Mother Cézanne because of the sordid stinginess prevailing in that house." Cézanne's bad temper and fear of people made him suspicious of even his most devoted friends, but they became used to his touchiness, so most did not bear grudges. They knew that underneath his gruff exterior there was a sensitive, insecure man.

INFLUENTIAL ASSESSMENTS

Towards the end of the 1880s, Cézanne was still only known by a small circle of avant-garde artists and critics. Nevertheless, interest in his work was increasing and by the early 1890s this

Right: Théodore Duret, *Manet, 1868.*
Duret was a businessman who later
became a journalist and art critic. An
admirer of the Impressionists, he actively
helped them by collecting their paintings.

was reinforced by further positive
reviews. In 1892, Émile Bernard
published a short biography of
Cézanne, and the French novelist,
playwright and critic George Lecomte
(1867–1958) gave a lecture about him
in Brussels, which was subsequently
published in his book, *L'Art
Impressioniste.* That year, the painter
Denis exhibited at the Salon and
announced that it was from "Monet,
Degas, Cézanne, Pissarro and Renoir…
that the younger artists borrowed their
art and vision…" The following year,
the critic Geffroy paid tribute to him in
several short appreciative articles.

SELLING CÉZANNE

In 1891, Cézanne's influential friend
Chocquet died. Tanguy died the
following year, which meant his painting

Above: Construction of the Eiffel Tower,
1889. At first hated by most Parisians, by
the 1890s the Eiffel Tower had become
an unmistakable symbol of Paris.

collection had to be sold. The following
March, the art critic Théodore Duret
(1838–1927) suffered considerable
business losses and was forced to sell a
large part of his art collection, which
contained three pictures by Cézanne.
These fetched fairly healthy prices of
between 600 and 800 francs. Tanguy's
collection was sold at an auction at the
Hôtel Drouot two months later, on
2 June 1894, and Vollard, who was
relatively unknown at the time, bought
six of Cézanne's paintings. After the
sale, Geffroy wrote a longer article in a
prestigious publication, *Le Journal,* solely
about Cézanne. It pointed out that,
although elusive and unfamiliar to the
public, he was a huge influence on
younger artists and should be
recognized for his innovative skills. That
year too, Caillebotte died suddenly at
the age of 46. In his will, he bequeathed
his large collection of paintings to the
nation. Horrified, Académie officials
tried to prevent the Impressionist
works from being thrust on them,
particularly those by Cézanne.

Left: Self-portrait, *Gustave Caillebotte,*
1889. This is a self-portrait of Caillebotte,
artist, collector and friend of the
Impressionists, who bequeathed his
art collection to the nation.

MONET

Cézanne spent most of the 1890s dividing his time, as he had done before, between Aix and Paris. He continued painting landscapes and figures in and around the Jas de Bouffan, as well as his still lifes and portraits.

In 1894, Cézanne went to Giverny for a short time. He stayed at the local inn and spent most of his time with Monet, which was the object of the visit. The two men highly esteemed each other's work and opinions.

SOCIALIZING WITH MONET

On 12 November 1894, Monet wrote to Geffroy: "Day after tomorrow, Wednesday, will be my birthday (fifty-four years); you would give me great pleasure if you could liberate yourself for that day and spend it here… you will meet Cézanne who arrived here a few days ago and who will be as happy to meet you as you'll be to get

MANET'S NIECE

On 18 March 1894, Duret's collection of paintings was auctioned at the Hôtel Drouot, fetching a record price of 160,000 francs. On the day before the sale, the 15-year-old daughter of Berthe Morisot and Manet's brother Eugène went to see the pictures and wrote in her diary: "…The one painter whom I like very much, from what I have seen of his here, is Cézanne; above all it's his well-modelled apples that I like (I only know these three paintings by him)."

acquainted with him." At the birthday celebration, Monet introduced Cézanne to the statesman Georges Clemenceau (1841–1929), the sculptor Auguste Rodin (1840–1917) and Geffroy. He was inordinately touched by the affection with which he was greeted, and a warm handshake from Rodin in Monet's garden moved him to tears. Years of shyness and insecurity were momentarily discarded and he happily joined in the revelry. Monet wrote to a

Below: Still Life with Apples, c.*1893–4. Cézanne often portrayed objects from more than one angle. Here, the ginger jar is depicted from two angles.*

Above: Cézanne in 1904. Cézanne's admirer Bernard took this photo of him on the hill at Les Lauves in Aix.

friend: "How unfortunate that this man should not have had more support in his existence. He is a true artist who has much too much self-doubt. He needs to be bolstered up…" In an effort to do so, Monet invited some other friends to Giverny and when they were all gathered, he declared to Cézanne: "At last we are here all together and happy to seize this occasion; to tell you how fond we all are of you and how much we admire your art." The response was not what he had anticipated. Cézanne stared at him for a moment and then burst out: "You too are making fun of me!" He snatched his coat and left.

THE INVENTOR OF IMPRESSIONISM

During Monet's birthday celebrations, the Impressionist painter Mary Cassatt (1844–1926) stayed at the same inn as Cézanne and talked to him there as well as at Monet's house. In a letter to a friend, she described him vividly: "The circle has been increased by a celebrity in the person of the first Impressionist, Monsieur Cézanne – 'the inventor of Impressionism'… When I first saw him, I thought he looked like a cut-throat with large red eyeballs standing out from his head in a most ferocious manner, a rather fierce-looking pointed

Top: The Card Players, 1890–2. Cézanne may have drawn inspiration for this work from a painting by the Le Nain brothers.

Above: The Large Pine, c.1889. This is reminiscent of a painting by Monet of a similar subject. Pines were a popular motif.

beard, quite grey, and an excited way of talking that positively made the dishes rattle. I found later on that I had misjudged his appearance, for far from fierce or a cut-throat, he has the gentlest nature possible, 'comme un enfant' as he would say. His manners at first rather startled me – he scrapes his soup plate, then lifts it and pours the

remaining drops in the spoon… he eats with his knife and accompanies every gesture, every movement of his hand with that implement… Yet in spite of the total disregard of the dictionary of manners, he shows a politeness toward us which no other man here would have shown… Cézanne is one of the most liberal artists I have ever met …."

ONE-MAN EXHIBITION

By November 1895, Vollard's gallery in the rue Lafitte was ready. For the opening he planned an exhibition of Cézanne's paintings, since Geffroy's favourable review in *Le Journal* had prompted public interest in his work.

Pissarro wrote to his son Lucien about Cézanne's first one-man exhibition: "… All of us, are we mistaken? I don't think so. The only ones who are not subject to Cézanne's charm are those artists and collectors who have shown by their errors of judgement that their sensibilities are defective…"

A FASCINATING SHOW

Cézanne proved difficult to locate and Vollard tried for months to secure his agreement to send 150 works for the exhibition. Eventually, through negotiations with his 23-year-old son Paul, the paintings were delivered and the exhibition opened on 7 November. However, even though it was Cézanne's first solo exhibition, he did not attend. The works were rotated over the two-month exhibition as there was not enough room in Vollard's small shop for them all to be seen at once. There were examples of Cézanne's paintings from his whole career, and they stimulated great interest and discussion.

Many visitors were still repulsed by these works, but at last, there were many others who were fascinated and inspired, and as a consequence, Vollard's reputation as an avant-garde dealer was immediately established. Pissarro, who had been one of the main instigators of the exhibition, was exceptionally enthusiastic about the work. He wrote to his eldest son Lucien: "How rarely do you come across true painters, who know how to balance two tones… Cézanne's show in which there are exquisite things, still lifes of irreproachable perfection, others, much worked on and yet

Above: The House with Cracked Walls, *1892–4. Cézanne carried the theme of cracked walls through the landscape with black lines in the forms of the tree trunks, in the path and in the markings on the rocks.*

Left: Portrait of Ambroise Vollard in a Red Scarf, Renoir, *c.1911. In contrast with his sittings for Cézanne, when posing for Renoir, Vollard was allowed to speak, move and relax.*

Right: Still Life with Statuette, *1894–5. The white statuette contrasts dramatically with colourful fruit and vegetables in this intricate composition of tilted lines and planes.*

unfinished, of even greater beauty, landscapes, nudes… But my enthusiasm was nothing compared to Renoir's. Degas himself is seduced by the charm of this refined savage… As Renoir said so well, these paintings have I do not know what quality, like the frescoes of Pompeii, so crude and so admirable!"

BUYING THE PAINTINGS

The Impressionists who had known Cézanne for 30 years had not been aware of the extent and depth of his work, as he had been so reticent at their café meetings and rarely invited people into his studio. They felt they were in the presence of a great master. Several of them bought his paintings, and Renoir and Degas even drew lots over a drawing that they both wanted. Pissarro, Monet and Vollard were incensed if critics did not share their enthusiasm; now, several warm articles appeared in the press along with the usual disrespectful ones. Yet Cézanne suffered deeply when he read any review of his work, as he was profoundly sensitive to the lack of understanding, so that even the positive reviews distressed him. In April 1896, he wrote: "I curse the Geffroys and the few rascals who, to write an article for 50 francs, drew the attention of the public to me. All my life I have worked to be able to earn my living, but I thought that one could do good painting without attracting attention to one's private life. To be sure, an artist wishes to raise himself intellectually as much as possible, but the man must remain obscure."

UNFINISHED PORTRAIT

Despite 'cursing the Geffroys', Cézanne agreed to paint Geffroy's portrait. Possibly inspired by a painting by Degas of Edmond Duranty from 1879, he surrounded the subject with the paraphernalia of his

Above: Riverbank, c.*1895. The primed white canvas shows through thinly washed pigments, while harmonies of colour unify the surface. All the colours have an equal intensity.*

occupation. But despite 80 sittings over a period of three months, he abandoned the painting before finishing it. Three weeks later, he wrote to

Monet: "I was forced to abandon for the time being the study that I had started at the house of Geffroy, who had placed himself so generously at my disposal, and I am a little upset at the meagre result I obtained, especially after so many sittings and successive bursts of enthusiasm and despair." Geffroy, on the other hand, thought it was one of Cézanne's finest works.

ESCAPING SOCIETY

Cézanne was still only 56, but he had aged prematurely, and his hair and beard were quite white. He was suffering from the ill-effects of diabetes, and this underlying malaise made him argumentative with everyone.

Above: Old Woman with a Rosary, *1895. It is believed that the sitter was a former nun who, at 70 years old, lost her faith. Cézanne took her on as a servant.*

Even though his work was beginning to receive recognition, he remained in mental turmoil, not trusting those around him, upsetting his friends and confining himself increasingly to Aix.

A NEW FRIEND

After spending the first six months of 1895 in Paris, Cézanne travelled to Aix and remained there for a whole year. In the spring of 1896, he was introduced to several new acquaintances in Aix,

Above: In the Park of the Château Noir, *c.1896–9. As Cézanne's style matured, he repeatedly painted one of several paintings of the mysterious Château Noir, using vivid orange-golds and contrasting cool greens.*

including the writer, poet and art critic Joachim Gasquet (1873–1921), who was the son of an old school friend. Unusually for Cézanne, he instantly bonded with Gasquet and treated

Above: Still Life with Onions, *c.1895. The bottle and glass mark the vertical axis of the composition, the edge of the table traces the horizontal line, while the diagonal knife, like an arrow, creates an illusion of depth.*

his young friend almost as a substitute for Zola, taking him to the same pine-clad foothills of the Mont Sainte-Victoire where he had spent so much time 40 years earlier with his former school friend. They visited the Château Noir, which appears in several of Cézanne's paintings of the period as a mysterious place, veiled with pine trees. Later, they went to Le Tholonet, another location that was much favoured by Cézanne and Zola. These were places he had not visited much for years and they gave him new inspiration for paintings.

Gasquet junior was among the few non-painters whom Cézanne permitted to watch him paint. In July of that year, he wrote to Gasquet, thanking him for allowing him to share in his 'adorable youth'. In turn, Gasquet introduced him to several other young poets and although Cézanne notoriously cherished solitude, he enjoyed the company of these sensitive and intelligent acquaintances – up to a point.

MEETING OLD FRIENDS

While in Aix, Cézanne also spent some time with his old school friends, local sculptor Philippe Solari (1840–1906), journalist Numa Coste (1843–1907) and Joachim's father, Henri Gasquet (c.1839–1906). Over the next year, Cézanne painted portraits of both father and son and, touched by Joachim's enthusiasm for his work, he gave Joachim one of his Mont Sainte-Victoire paintings. Occasionally, he went to the Café Oriental on the cours Mirabeau in Aix, where he met another old friend, a novelist, journalist and close friend of Zola's, Paul Alexis (1847–1901).

During the spring of 1896, for the first time, the gallery owner Ambroise Vollard travelled to Aix to meet Cézanne. Before that time, all his negotiations had been conducted through Cézanne's son. During his stay, as well as discussing another solo exhibition, he bought paintings that Cézanne had given to various residents of Aix.

Right: Man Smoking a Pipe, *1890–2.*
Cézanne painted three versions of the same farm labourer from the Jas de Bouffan, leaning on his elbow and smoking a white clay pipe.

PAINTING AS A DIVERSION

Even though he socialized more, Cézanne made it clear to friends and family that he preferred solitude, so that in the main, others respected his wishes and left him to it. In May, Zola wrote a review of the Salon in *Le Figaro*. He made it clear that he was completely alienated from the Impressionists by that time. He expressed disillusionment with their art and he labelled Cézanne 'an abortive genius'. He also stayed for a few days with Numa Coste in Aix, but made no attempt to contact Cézanne while there. Perhaps because of these events, Cézanne felt ill and travelled to the spa town of Vichy in south-eastern France, where he spent the month of June. For the whole of July, at the request of Hortense and Paul, he once again returned to Switzerland, this time to Talloires on the shore of the Lac d'Annecy, where he captured the tranquil views with one oil painting and a series of watercolours. Since his falling-out with Zola, he no longer penned so many regular, candid letters, but he did still write to some people, including his childhood friend, Solari. From Switzerland, he wrote: "I paint to divert myself; it is not very amusing, but the lake is very nice with the big mountains all round..." Taking a long route home, by late August he was in Paris looking for a studio that suited him. He found one in Montmartre, on the rue des Dames, and remained there until winter.

ART AND NATURE

Dismayed once more by the criticism of him in Zola's latest article, Cézanne distanced himself from all contact with his friends, painting feverishly and spending much of his time caring for his elderly and frail mother.

Although Gasquet reported that Zola always spoke of Cézanne with "the most affectionate admiration", it is not clear exactly what Zola did feel for his old friend, and conflicting reports abound.

FRIENDS AND RELATIONS
According to Gasquet, Zola said he always felt, "in spite of his sulkiness, all the friendship of a big, fraternal heart". Despite his pointedly derogatory writings, he also said of Cézanne's work, "I begin to better understand his painting, which I have always liked but which for a long time I did not understand, for I thought it exaggerated, whereas actually it is unbelievably sincere and truthful." Yet he never tried to renew their friendship. Meanwhile, Cézanne continued to work for long hours each day, except for the entire month of January in 1897, when he was bedridden with flu. By this time,

Below: The Smoker, *c.1895–1900. When he painted peasants relaxing and smoking, Cézanne concentrated on the colouring and form of each figure.*

Cézanne and Hortense had grown apart. Their son had grown up and so they had few reasons to speak. Whatever love they had felt for each other when they first met had long vanished. She no longer modelled patiently for her husband, and in her place he occasionally employed a model called Marie-Louise for his later figurative paintings. He remained fearful and suspicious of most women.

AVOIDING MODERNITY
In Paris, in February, a new annexe of the Musée du Luxembourg opened, housing the Caillebotte bequest. It was not only the art officials who had protested over this; there had been a general public outcry, and a large number of politicians and critics had also voiced their protests. When the much-reduced collection was displayed, yet again Cézanne's art was received with contempt. From his distance in Aix, this did not hurt as much as in the past, especially as others were interested in his work by then,

but it still affected his mood. Cézanne remained in Aix, mainly to care for his mother. He no longer returned to L'Estaque, since the building of a mineral plant there had ruined the picturesque qualities for him, and he rarely went to Paris, because city life did not inspire him. Whereas the Impressionists and most of the Post-Impressionists were fascinated with modernity and featured it frequently in their works, Cézanne abhorred it, preferring to convey an enduring quality.

SHOCKING NATURE INTO PERMANENCE
Cézanne actively sought timelessness in his paintings of bathers. He did not aim to appeal to those who were simply looking for beauty in art, but tried to reinterpret a long tradition of paintings

Below: Bathers, *c.1892–4. Cézanne produced several small paintings of bathers. The brushstrokes seem sketchy and spontaneous, but each picture was carefully composed and every mark was planned.*

'MINUTE SENSATION'

As Cézanne's art developed through his life, he remained faithful to his aim of capturing what he called his 'minute sensation'. He only reached this after hours of observation and he would not even begin a work until he had decided how he would capture it. His admirers recognized this; those who did not understand his work could not see it. More than atmosphere, it was the entire essence of the motif. His 'sensation' was not a passive 'impression', but was seen by the eye and then organized by the mind.

Left: Standing Nude Woman, c.1898–9. *This is Marie-Louise, the model he occasionally used in later life, painted in Cézanne's Montmartre studio. "The culmination of art is the figure," he once said to Vollard.*

nature into permanence… Art must make nature eternal in our imagination." His paintings of bathers embodied his ideas of permanence in nature. Over time, the water gradually disappeared from the scenes and the figures became more dominant within their surroundings.

with nude figures in the landscape by artists such as Titian and Poussin. He constructed his paintings using his knowledge of colour, solid forms and structures. He explained: "I have all the parts of my canvas under control simultaneously. If things are tending to diverge, I use my instincts and beliefs to bring them back together again… Nature is always the same, even though its visible manifestations eventually cease to exist. Our art must shock

Right: Cézanne Painting a View from Les Lauves, Maurice Denis, 1906. *In the year of Cézanne's death, Denis created this picture of his hero painting in the open air. Denis himself is seated on the ground to the right, making a sketch for this work.*

CHANGES

In October 1897, 83-year-old Anne-Elisabeth-Honorine Cézanne died. It was a sad time for
Cézanne, who had been extremely close to his mother throughout his life, and had looked
after her during her last years.

Since 1891, Cézanne had been a
devout Catholic, which gave him some
comfort, although he described Mass
to his friend Alexis as "a slice of the
Middle Ages". In the same way that
his dealings with his family and friends
were sometimes difficult, Cézanne's
relationship with his religion was not
simple or straightforward.

CATHOLICISM

In 1891, Cézanne told Alexis that he
had returned to the Church out of the
fear of death, but he hated priests and
was afraid of getting into their "clutches".
He said, "I think that to be a Catholic
one must be devoid of all sense of
justice, but have a good eye for one's
interest." Yet Catholicism also gave
him a feeling of security. He explained
in a letter to his niece: "Once we have

reached a certain age, we find no
other support and consolation than
in religion."

SETTLING THE ESTATE

Within two years of his mother's death,
on the instigation of Maxime Conil, it
was decided that the Jas de Bouffan
should be sold to consolidate the
estate. Conil was a gambler and
permanently in debt. He had sold
Bellevue in 1899, the property he and
Rose owned; he took her share of the
sale of the Jas de Bouffan – 33,000
francs – in 1899, and the following
month he also sold two paintings to
Vollard that Cézanne had given Rose
as a gift. Although by then, Cézanne
could have paid for his sisters' shares
of the Jas de Bouffan with his father's
inheritance and the awakening interest

Above: Château Noir, *1904–6. This is
one of four oil paintings of Château Noir.
All four are dark in tone, the crumbling
façade of the building looming above the
dense foliage in greens and purples that
contrast with the orange of the building.*

in his work, he decided not to. He
probably weighed the cost of the
upkeep of the estate against his fond
memories of it and decided it was time
to move on. By the time of his mother's
death, Hortense and Paul spent most of
their time in Paris; Hortense gambled
and frequently overspent and Cézanne
lived a modest and solitary life, so the
farm was not a practical proposition.
Hortense had never lived there, as she
had fallen out with Cézanne's family,
and she always claimed to hate the
place. Leaving the home that he had

been so attached to, however, was a great strain. Not only did he love all it meant to him, but most of all, it had afforded him seclusion and a peaceful atmosphere in which to paint. He had never adapted well to new environments and now that he was older and suffering with diabetes and other physical problems, moving away proved even more stressful.

CHÂTEAU NOIR

Once the Jas de Bouffan was sold, Cézanne rented an apartment on the rue de Boulegon in Aix, where he was cared for by his faithful housekeeper, who had been at the Jas de Bouffan. He also rented a cabin in the Bibémus Quarry, which he had used a few years before, and a small room in the Château Noir, a large house between Aix and Le Tholonet. In contrast to the well-maintained trees and gardens at the Jas de Bouffan, the grounds of the Château Noir were wild and unkempt, and its dense pine wood created an atmosphere that Cézanne had not experienced at the more open Jas de Bouffan. As well as the light effects and bold colours of the location, the Château Noir had a mysterious and appealing history. It was built by a coal merchant in the late 19th century. It was believed that the owner had originally painted it black to match his profession, so it became known as the 'Black House'. In fact, it was never painted and always bore the bright orange colour of the Bibémus Quarry limestone from which it was made. Another story was that its first owner was a crazed alchemist who was involved with the devil; a more sinister nickname for the house was 'Château du Diable' (House of the Devil).

Above right: Mont Sainte-Victoire, *1902–6. With small coloured patches, Cézanne emphasized the painted surface by bringing the background and middleground forward.*

Right: Still Life with Curtain, *c.1899. The complex arrangement of fruit, dishes, jug and drapery on a table is given stability by the bold forms of the white cloth.*

Entranced by its legends as much as the light and colours surrounding it, Cézanne offered to buy the Château Noir, but the owner would not sell it.

Right: Mont Sainte-Victoire above the Route du Tholonet, *1896–8. In the late 1890s, Cézanne returned to many sites of his youth around Le Tholonet. Here he has placed the mountain close to the top of his canvas in order to feature more of the landscape below.*

LAST WORKS

Once Cézanne learned that he could not purchase the Château Noir, he bought a piece of land to the north of Aix called Les Lauves, and within three years, he had built a studio there. Here he painted his favourite themes with unflagging concentration.

From his new studio at Les Lauves, he tirelessly painted still lifes, figures and landscapes, with views of Mont Sainte-Victoire continuing to dominate.

PUBLIC APPRECIATION

Chocquet had died in 1891. After the death of his widow in 1899, 32 of his Cézanne paintings were sold, making over 51,000 francs in total. Most of the paintings were bought by Paul Durand-Ruel (1831–1922), the Impressionists' main dealer, who had not previously bought many works by Cézanne. Monet insisted that Durand-Ruel should take an interest in Cézanne, so he bought 17 works at the Chocquet sale. A year later, he sent 12 of the paintings to Germany for the first exhibition of Cézanne's work to be held there. None of the works sold, but interest in his work was aroused.

At the end of 1899, Vollard wrote to Gauguin in Tahiti: "I have purchased all of Cézanne's paintings that were in his studio. I have already held three or four exhibitions of them; they are beginning to catch on with the public." The following year, in 1900, another Exposition Universelle was held in Paris to celebrate the achievements of the past century. Over 50,000,000 visitors attended to marvel at recent inventions such as films and escalators, as well as a centennial exhibition of French art. Three of Cézanne's works were included. Additionally, in 1901, he finally agreed to submit work to the exhibition of the Société des Artistes Indépendants, having previously refused to participate for some years. He also exhibited again with Les XX in Brussels, and in 1904 he was given an entire room at the Salon d'Automne.

HOMAGE TO CÉZANNE

In 1901, Maurice Denis exhibited a painting at the Salon entitled *Homage to Cézanne*. It depicts a group of artists and friends, including Denis, Redon, Édouard Vuillard (1868–1940), Pierre Bonnard (1867–1947), Vollard and others, admiring a still life, *Fruit Bowl, Glass and Apples* by Cézanne, that had belonged to Gauguin. Public reaction to the work was a mixture of hostility and appreciation. One reviewer explained: "Cézanne is not known to the masses… but for a number of years, painters have been following him attentively."

It was Denis who convinced Cézanne to exhibit again with the Société des Artistes Indépendants in 1902. He had warm feelings toward these "young people who have shown themselves to be so much in sympathy with me", and he wrote to Vollard, asking him to send Denis the works "that are calculated to do the least harm".

Left: Young Italian Girl Resting on Her Elbow, *c.1900. Featuring a piece of carpet used often by Cézanne, aspects of this young woman's portrait clearly influenced later artists including Picasso and Modigliani.*

Right: Chrysanthemums, c.1896–1900. *With hindsight, it is apparent in this expressive painting that Cézanne inspired several modern art movements of the 20th century.*

FINAL STRUGGLES

As Cézanne slowly achieved recognition, he began concentrating on even fewer themes than before and leaving Aix even less. Among his favourite subjects were the Mont Sainte-Victoire, bathers, still lifes and portraits of local workers. His later painting style became particularly innovative, built up of separated brush marks. These marks are nothing like his earlier blended colour forms; however, his approach remained the same. He still contemplated his subject for a long time before painting, trying to understand his sensation of it. Cézanne's dedication to his art accelerated his death. He was now in weakening health, and on 15 October 1906 he was caught in a storm when out painting. He lost consciousness and was carried home. He died from pneumonia eight days later, on 23 October 1906.

Below right: Cézanne in his studio in 1904. Cézanne was never satisfied with his work. In 1905 he lamented, "My age and my health will never allow me to realize the artistic dream I have pursued throughout my entire life."

PORTRAIT OF VOLLARD

At the end of 1899, four years after he had abandoned the portrait of Geffroy, Cézanne was commissioned to paint a portrait of Ambroise Vollard. Vollard sat 117 times for him, from 8 a.m. until 11.30 a.m. He liked to tell others about Cézanne's nervousness, concentration and need for complete silence. After the 117th sitting, Cézanne stopped working, leaving two unexplained white spots of bare canvas on Vollard's right hand. He claimed that he was "not discontented with the front of the shirt".

Above: Landscape at Aix (Mont Sainte-Victoire), *1905. Cézanne's studio at Les Lauves had a large window that overlooked Aix. He had a clear view of Mont Sainte-Victoire.*

THE GALLERY

From the moment in the 1850s that Cézanne decided he wanted to become a painter, he remained resolute. No matter how difficult things became, even when he was persistently ridiculed and criticized, he tenaciously worked to achieve his aims, to find a way of capturing his 'minute sensations'. His struggles in the face of self-doubt, paternal resistance and his difficult personality have made him a legendary figure who personifies our image of an artist striving against all odds for his art. Yet he was a sensitive, well-educated and thoughtful man and his potential was always recognized by a few. His style changed quite dramatically over his career, from his early dark canvases to the luminous paintings that gave new dimensions to Impressionism and finally to his ground-breaking later works that affected art for the following century.

Left: Plate of Peaches, *1879, oil on canvas, Guggenheim Museum, New York, NY, USA, 59.7 x 73.3cm (23 x 28in).*

A SEARCH FOR DIRECTION

Largely untutored in art, Cézanne made up his own rules. When he first began painting, he learned some traditional techniques at his local municipal art college, but prior to that, he had not shown any specific artistic skills and his imagination had been fired by writers. A proud and introspective young man, by 1859 he had decided that painting was to be his vocation and from then on, he worked unceasingly to achieve his goals. His early works, with their often violent, sensual and morbid themes in dark tones with heavily loaded brush marks attracted acerbic and derisive comments from his friends, neighbours and critics.

Above: Jourdan's Hut, *1906, oil on canvas, Galleria Nazionale d'Arte Moderna, Rome, Italy, 65 x 82cm (25 x 32in).*
Left: Auvers-sur-Oise, Seen from the Val Harme, *1879–82, oil on canvas, Private Collection, Switzerland, 73 x 92cm (28 x 36in).*

*The Dream of the Poet or the
Kiss of the Muse,* 1859–60,
oil on canvas,
Musée Granet,
Aix-en-Provence, France,
82 x 66cm (32 x 26in)

Cézanne's earliest works
were inspired by Renaissance
masters. Using smooth
gradations of paint, he built
up the impression of drapery
in an attempt to interpret a
mythological story that
symbolizes his own dreams
of becoming an artist. His
classical approach evolved
from the methods he was
learning at the Municipal
School of Drawing in Aix.

*Interior with Two Women
and a Child,* 1860–2,
oil on canvas, Pushkin
State Museum of Fine
Art, Moscow, Russia,
91 x 72cm (35 x 28in)

This is another work that
demonstrates Cézanne's
newly learned skills from his
studies in Aix. The subject is
believed to have been taken
from the women's magazines
that his sisters subscribed to.
In contrast with the smooth
modulations of *The Dream of
the Poet,* this was created
with round brushes, using
the stark contrasts
of the black background
and bold colours to
create a completely
different style of work.

Spring and Autumn,
1859–62, oil on canvas,
Musée du Petit Palais,
Paris, France,
315 x 98cm (124 x 38in)

When the family moved
into the Jas de Bouffan,
Louis-Auguste allowed

Cézanne to decorate the
salon. In a classical style,
revealing his natural drawing
skills and good handling of
colour gradations, he
painted four elegant panels
depicting the seasons. The
elongated paintings were
acquired by Vollard in 1899.

Head of an Old Man, c.1866, oil on canvas, Musée d'Orsay, Paris, France, 51 x 48cm (20 x 18in)

With a palette knife and occasionally a brush, Cézanne has built up a heavy impasto application, creating strong tonal contrasts and rich textures to capture the man's gentle expression. Hinting of his later interests, the modelling shows a concentrated expression of the man's dome-like skull. The clothes are painted roughly and robustly, but they are not finished, revealing that this work was painted over a previous painting.

Dominique Aubert, the Artist's Uncle, as a Monk, 1866, oil on canvas, Metropolitan Museum of Art, New York, NY, USA, 65 x 55cm (26 x 22in)

This painting of Cézanne's maternal uncle, Dominique Aubert, is one of at least nine portraits of him that Cézanne painted in the autumn of 1866. The 49-year-old bailiff not only indulged his nephew with many sittings but also agreed to pose in various costumes, such as this one of a Dominican monk. The paint was applied so thickly that cracks emerged almost as soon as it dried.

The Painter's Father, Louis-Auguste Cézanne, c.1860, **black and white photograph.**

Louis-Auguste was in his early 60s, and his son was 20, when this photograph was taken of him. At that time, Cézanne was in conflict with his father over his future career. Louis-Auguste wanted his son to continue studying law, but Paul begged his mother to help convince his father that his true path was to study art in Paris. The next year, his father gave in to the inevitable and Paul Cézanne went to Paris.

La Toilette (Ladies Dressing), c.1864–8, oil on canvas, Private Collection, 22 x 33cm (8 x 13in)

By the mid-1860s, Cézanne was profoundly inspired by the writings of Flaubert and the paintings of Delacroix, and taking some of their ideas; he combined traditional and contemporary ideas within one composition. The results were often rather macabre images that he later described as "gutsy" (*couillard*), given their forceful character. Using sweeping brushstrokes, another clear influence here is the wall paintings of ancient Greece and Rome.

*The Feast, c.*1867–72, oil on canvas, Private Collection, 130 x 81cm (51 x 31in)

"My hair is longer than my talent," Cézanne complained in his 20s. His determination to improve meant that he spent every day working at his art. By the 1870s, his compositional skills began emerging. This large work thrusts the action instantly into the viewer's vision, with diagonals dominating and figures overlapping and interrelating almost violently. Colours are simultaneously vivid and subtle.

Christ in Limbo, 1867, oil on canvas, Musée d'Orsay, Paris, France, 170 x 97cm (67 x 38in)

This is the left-hand fragment of a larger canvas. It was originally connected to Mary Magdalene (see opposite page), even though the styles and proportions of the two works are totally different. It is based on a painting by the Renaissance artist, Sebastiano del Piombo (c.1485–1547). Christ is descending into Limbo after his death and before his resurrection. It is created with impasto paint in muted colours and broad brushstrokes.

Mary Magdalene, c.1867,
oil on canvas, Musée
d'Orsay, Paris, France,
165 x 123cm (65 x 48in)

Part of a much larger work
and probably intended to
decorate the Jas de Bouffan,
this painting reflects both
Cézanne's religious beliefs
and Provençal traditions. In a
medieval legend, Mary
Magdalene ended her days
near the Mont Sainte-
Victoire. The style was
probably inspired by the
Italian Baroque painter
Domenico Fetti (*c.*1589-
1623), whose work Cézanne
saw in the Louvre.

Portrait of Fortuné Marion,
1867–8, oil on canvas,
Kunstmuseum,
Basel, Switzerland,
60 x 50cm (23 x 19in)

An old school friend of
Cézanne's, Antoine Fortuné
Marion was a naturalist who
painted in his spare time and
admired Cézanne from the
start of his painting career.
This portrait was captured
quickly and smoothly, with
paint thickly applied using
palette knives. With its
strong composition and tonal
contrasts, it shows Spanish
Master influences, while
remaining creatively
independent, forceful
and immediate.

Still Life with Green Pot and Pewter Jug, c.1867–9, oil on canvas, Musée d'Orsay, Paris, France, 65 x 81cm (26 x 32in)

Remaining interested in still lifes throughout his life, Cézanne's early paintings in this genre are skilful, showing his understanding of colour and his ability to create a sense of stability and calm. With his first still lifes, such as this one, he used thick paint, strong colours and a lot of black; methods inspired by Old Masters.

Young Girl at the Piano, Overture to Tannhäuser, c.1868–70, oil on canvas, Hermitage Museum, St Petersburg, Russia, 57 x 92cm (22 x 36in)

Inspired by Wagner's overture to *Tannhäuser,* Cézanne painted his youngest sister Rose at the piano and his mother sewing in the background. He gave the painting to Rose on her marriage to Maxime Conil in 1881. Years later, Conil sold it to Vollard. Tannhäuser is a German love story. Fortuné Marion wrote about the work: "…it belongs to the future as much as Wagner's music".

The Murder, c.1867, oil on canvas, Walker Art Gallery, Liverpool, UK, 65 x 81cm (26 x 32in)

This shows Cézanne's early fascination with the great artists of the past, such as Géricault and Vélazquez. In the brutal image, the murderer is lifting his hand ready to give the final blow while his collaborator holds the victim down. All three figures' identities are anonymous and the crime is not explained. The menacing sky and the desolate surroundings add to the ominous atmosphere.

Portrait of Achille Emperaire,
1867–8, oil on canvas,
Musée d'Orsay,
Paris, France,
200 x 120cm (78 x 47in)

This life-sized portrait of
Cézanne's friend and fellow
artist from Aix exaggerates
his deformities. In 1870, this
work was rejected from the
Salon, and late in life
Cézanne wanted to destroy
it. When he painted it, his
emphasis was on its huge
format, the stately chair and
the inscription, all of which
echoed Ingres' painting
of Napoleon I on the
Imperial Throne.

Alexis Reading to Zola,
c.1867–9, oil on canvas,
Private Collection,
Switzerland,
52 x 56cm (20 x 22in)

Paul Alexis was one of
Cézanne's and Zola's
childhood friends from Aix.
He later became a novelist,
dramatist and journalist, and
in 1882 wrote a biography
of Zola. This was the first
version that Cézanne
painted of this scenario, the
second is below. He used
some 17th-century Dutch
painting techniques, including
framing the picture with a
curtain and illuminating a
dark interior with light from
a window.

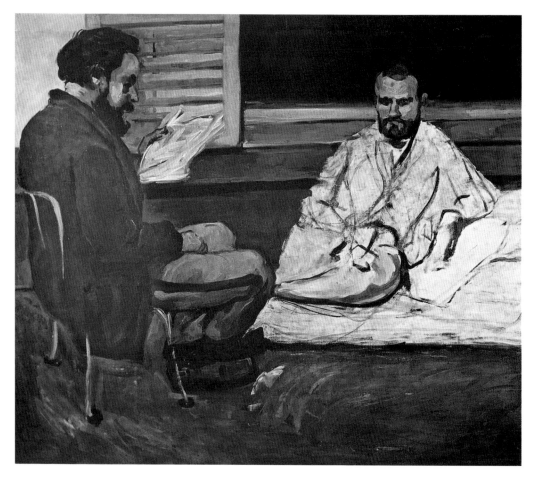

*Paul Alexis Reading a
Manuscript to Émile Zola,*
1869–70, oil on canvas,
Museu de Arte,
São Paulo, Brazil,
130 x 160cm (51 x 63in)

This was the second version
of the painting above.
For a short time, Alexis
was Zola's secretary. While
most of the rest of the
canvas is complete, Zola's
figure remains a bare patch
of canvas with a few lines
sketched in black paint to
mark the folds of his clothes.
It seems he found it difficult
to complete any likeness of
his closest friend.

Still Life with Pot, Bottle, Cup and Fruit, c.1869–71, oil on canvas, Nationalgalerie, Staatliche Museen zu Berlin, Germany, 64 x 80cm (25 x 31in)

Throughout his career, Cézanne remained interested in the still life. From his early works to his later paintings, these are all remarkably well composed; dynamic yet with great stability, with dense tones and a richness of colour and contrast. Still lifes like this remained a constant throughout his life and can be compared with each other in order to understand how his individual style developed from the start.

The Black Clock, 1869–70, oil on canvas, Private Collection, France, 55 x 74cm (22 x 29in)

The black clock, painted without hands, belonged to Zola. The tablecloth falls in deep folds and the objects on it are reminiscent of 17th-century Dutch still lifes. The richly shaped contours and clearly expressed textures show an architectural understanding of balance and harmony, emphasised by the rococo-style fluting of the conch shell and vase, the half-hidden curves of the lemon and the straight lines of the cup and clock.

Railroad Cutting with Mont Sainte-Victoire, 1870, oil on canvas, Neue Pinakothek, Munich, Germany, 80 x 129cm (31 x 51in)

Close observation of nature became more important to Cézanne by the early 1870s, largely due to the conversations he was involved with at the Café Guerbois. He soon began to dispense with emotional scenes and to concentrate on painting from nature. This objective work focuses on the railway cutting and is his first painting to feature the Mont Sainte-Victoire.

Melting Snow, L'Estaque, 1870, oil on canvas, Private Collection, Switzerland, 73 x 95cm (28 x 37in)

In a rare painting of snow, Cézanne studied a landscape in a state of change. The subject and the long brushstrokes are reminiscent of the dramatic, emotional style of his early figure paintings. With fairly thick, fluid paint and strong colour, including ochre, black, Prussian blue, light red and white, it is striking and very different from the work his friends at the Café Guerbois were producing.

Faun Playing a Flute, after Coysevox, 1870, pencil on paper, Philadelphia Museum of Art, PA, USA, 18 x 12cm (7 x 5in)

Sketched from a sculpture by Charles-Antoine Coysevox (1640–1720), this shows Cézanne's flexible handling of graphite pencil using a minimum of lines and no superfluous details or tones. He preferred to work from sculpture rather than from life models and later claimed that most of his figures in his extensive bather paintings came from the sculptures he studied in museums over the course of his career.

Madame du Barry, after Pajou, c.1870–90, pencil on paper, Philadelphia Museum of Art, PA, USA, 18 x 12cm (7 x 5in)

As with all Cézanne's work, this is not dated; it is from a sketchbook that he took with him to the Louvre.

Madame Jeanne du Barry, a young and vivacious beauty, was the last mistress of Louis XV. Nearly 20 years after his death, she was guillotined. Cézanne drew this from the marble bust of her by Augustin Pajou (1730–1809) in the Louvre.

Countryside, c.1872, oil on board laid down on panel, Private Collection, 37 x 41cm (15 x 16in)

Cézanne had benefited greatly from time spent with Pissarro in Pontoise, and in September 1872, Pissarro wrote to Guillemet: "Our friend Cézanne raises our expectations and I have seen and have at home a painting of remarkable vigour and power. If, as I hope, he stays some time in Auvers where he is going to live, he will astonish a lot of artists who were too hasty in condemning him."

Quai de Bercy – La Halle aux Vins, 1872, oil on canvas, Portland Art Museum, OR, USA, 73 x 92cm (28 x 36in)

For a while, Cézanne lived in a second-floor apartment on the Left Bank in Paris. From his window, he could see this busy wine depot. Achille Emperaire described the noise from it as causing "enough uproar to wake the dead." Yet in Cézanne's predominantly monochrome painting, the place looks deserted.

*Landscape in the Swamps – near Melun, c.*1872, watercolour on paper, Private Collection, 31 x 48cm (12 x 18in)

In comparison to his oil paintings, Cézanne's watercolours are soft and ethereal. Most of them were studies for his oil paintings, but many were not developed into finished oil paintings. If he created a finished painting out of this, he must have destroyed it – as he did with many works.

*The Road, c.*1871, oil on canvas, Kunstmuseum, Basel, Switzerland, 60 x 72cm (24 x 28in)

Cézanne's landscape painting progressed in the 1870s. He continued using palette knives and thick paint in the manner of Courbet, with colours and compositions reminiscent of Corot or Granet. His first rural paintings do not emanate atmosphere, but the objectivity with which he painted them moves away from his earlier emotional works.

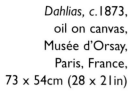

Dahlias, c.1873,
oil on canvas,
Musée d'Orsay,
Paris, France,
73 x 54cm (28 x 21in)

Cézanne exhibited three
still lifes and three flower
paintings at the third
Impressionist exhibition. This
was one of the flower
paintings that he painted
while staying with Dr Gachet
in Auvers – using one of
Madame Gachet's Delft
vases. Pissarro had
encouraged him to
paint flowers indoors as a
way of disciplining himself by
using smaller brush marks
and a brighter palette than
he had previously.

*Still Life with Pears and Green
Apples, c.1873–7,*
oil on canvas, Musée de
l'Orangerie, Paris, France,
22 x 32cm (8 x 12in)

From the early to mid-1870s
– and beyond – Cézanne
painted fruit repeatedly, using
a variety and intensity of
colour that he had not
exploited previously. This
particular work shows
some of the changes that
had occurred in his style
since he began working with
Pissarro. The application is
softer and shadows, rather
than being predominantly
black, now feature blends
and accents of colour.

Green Apples, c.1873, oil on canvas, Musée d'Orsay, Paris, France, 26 x 32cm (10 x 12in)

Cézanne famously declared, "I want to amaze Paris with an apple!" He meant that, rather than producing traditional art with nudes and stories from the Bible or mythology, he was going to create a new, revolutionary art form. One of his chosen subjects was still lifes, especially of fruit. Although fruit are simple objects, his paintings of them became progressively more intricate.

Déjeuner sur l'Herbe, c.1873–7, oil on canvas, Musée de l'Orangerie, Paris, France, 21 x 27cm (8 x 10in)

Cézanne had been so taken with Manet's painting of this title that he painted his own interpretations. This distinctive and dramatic composition contrasts strongly with Manet's work and with his own, earlier version. Here, he used his brighter Impressionistic palette and his angled brush marks. Because of the agitated brushstrokes across the canvas, it is difficult to identify the relationships between the figures.

IMPRESSIONISM

From the time he stayed with Pissarro in Pontoise, Cézanne seemed composed and content that he had found what he had anxiously been searching for. Although his approach and methods changed from that time, he did not follow Impressionism exactly, but used aspects of it for his own aims. The countryside of Pontoise and Oise, the discussions in Paris with other artists at the Café Guerbois, the landscape and light at L'Estaque and Aix, and perhaps most of all, his work with Pissarro, contributed to his development. For about a decade, he produced work that has since been described as his 'Impressionist phase': with a lighter, brighter palette and colour laid on his canvases in small, hatched brushstrokes.

Above: Apples and Cakes, *1877–9, oil on canvas, Private Collection, 46 x 55cm (18 x 21in).*
Left: Landscape in the Valley of the Oise, *1874–5, oil on canvas, Private Collection, 74 x 93cm (29 x 36in).*

Detour in Auvers, c.1873,
oil on canvas, Tokyo Fuji
Art Museum, Japan,
60 x 49cm (24 x 19 in)

Taking compositional ideas
from Pissarro, Cézanne leads
viewers' eyes round a bend
in the road, through some
trees and toward some
houses nestling together.
The interesting perspective
and the device of leading
the eye became a
composition that fascinated
Cézanne during that period.
Pissarro's style of painting is
apparent here, with the
gently curving tree branches
and small dabs of paint
across the entire canvas.

Quai de Bercy, c.1877, oil
on canvas, Kunsthalle,
Hamburg, Germany,
59 x 72cm (23 x 28in)

In spite of his apparent
adoption of the Impressionist
style, Cézanne was opposed
to the delicacy and lightness
of most of the works. To
show how he felt, he copied
one of his friend Guillaumin's
paintings, *The Seine at Bercy,*
of 1873–5, using stronger
colours and contrasts of
tone, enlarging the figures
and objects and firming up
the clouds, to create a more
distinct composition.

House and Tree near the Road of the Hermitage, 1873, oil on canvas, Private Collection, 65 x 54cm (25 x 21in)

Cézanne worked feverishly during the 1870s. He was inspired by the words of the 'humble and colossal' Pissarro as he called him. With a lightened palette, he applied tiny patches of colour to describe this view of a house and tree in Pontoise. His first layers of paint were applied with small daubs of colour that now included rich greens, blue-violet, yellow and orange.

Portrait of Camille Pissarro, c.1873, pencil on paper, Private Collection, 10 x 8cm (4 x 3in)

A great many of Cézanne's socializing problems stemmed from his shyness. So when he became close to Pissarro, he found it difficult to tell him how he wanted him to pose and drew him either from the back or from the side as here. This was never going to be worked into a full portrait, but it shows the affection Cézanne had for the sensitive older artist.

Bouquet with Yellow Dahlia, c.1873, oil on canvas, Musée d'Orsay, Paris, France, 54 x 64cm (21 x 25 in)

While staying at Dr Gachet's house, Cézanne painted several still lifes. This incorporates the same tablecloth and similar motifs as those in a painting by Guillaumin that was also painted in Gachet's house at around the same time. With thick, smooth paint and careful use of darks and lights, this work combines aspects of 17th-century Dutch still life and Impressionism.

Bouquet with Small Delft Vase, 1873, oil on canvas, Musée d'Orsay, Paris, France, 41 x 27cm (16 x 10in)

In 1914, Wassily Kandinsky (1866–1944) wrote *The Art of Spiritual Harmony.* In it, he said of Cézanne: "He turned a cup of tea into a being with a soul or, more precisely, he perceived life in this cup. He raised still life to the rank of an externally dead but internally living object... he had the gift of being able to discover inner life in everything."

The House of Dr Gachet at Auvers, 1873, oil on canvas, Kunstmuseum, Basel, Switzerland, 56 x 47cm (22 x 18in)

Cézanne was happy in Auvers and he painted Gachet's house several times.

In this work, the house is seen from an adjacent hill. Dr Gachet's house is behind the trees in the centre of the scene. The foreground is dominated by a wide green area and the painting is created in browns, greens and shades of white.

View of Auvers, 1873–4, oil on canvas, Art Institute of Chicago, IL, USA, 65 x 81cm (26 x 32in)

This work is evocative of Pissarro's paintings. Probably painted in 1873, Cézanne achieved this view from one of the hills around Auvers, so he could look down on the rooftops. He was influenced by Impressionism here, but was also showing signs of his future investigations into structure by interlocking the buildings and vegetation. It is one of the few works where he also made a feature of atmospheric perspective.

Crossroads at rue Rémy,
*c.*1873, oil on canvas, Musée
d'Orsay, Paris, France,
38 x 46cm (15 x 18in)

Cézanne's art had been
influenced by Impressionism
in Pontoise and then in
Auvers. But he never
tried to dissolve forms in
the shimmering light and
atmosphere as the
Impressionists did. Instead,
by juxtaposing rather grainy
brushstrokes, he gave solid
structure to all elements
within the landscape,
creating density and depth.
His strong composition here
focuses on the geometric
forms of the buildings.

*A View of Auvers, c.*1873–4,
oil on canvas,
Private Collection,
46 x 38cm (18 x 15in)

Declaring that he was
"striving for perfection,"
Cézanne used a soft yet
bright palette, involving
pinks, greens, blues, whites
and yellows. He had learned
that colour is contained in
reflections and it is also
created between eye and
object, so altering his
marks and consistency of
paint once again, he
applied daubs, small
blobs and patches, to
interpret and build up
the play of sunlight
across the landscape.

Studies; Faces and Figures,
1873, pencil on paper,
Szepmüveszeti Muzeum,
Budapest, Hungary,
22 x 29cm (9 x 11in)

During his career, Cézanne
produced more than
18 sketchbooks, filling their
pages with an almost
obsessive examination of
everything around him.
Not every drawing was
developed into a finished
painting and these studies
consist of disparate elements
on a single page, indicating
that they were meant to
be just that; studies and not
a complete composition.
There is no thematic
consistency; but at least
one of the faces seems to
be that of Hortense.

*Still Life with Italian
Earthenware Jar,*
1872–3, oil on canvas,
Private Collection,
40 x 55cm (15 x 20in)

Retaining the bright colours
of Impressionism, but
beginning to abandon the
atmospheric tones in favour
of the intensity of local
colour, this work
was painted while
Cézanne was staying
with Dr Gachet
and searching
for a new mode
of expression.

Lake at the Jas de Bouffan, 1873–6, oil on canvas, Sheffield Galleries and Museums Trust, UK, 46 x 56cm (18 x 22in)

The two years he spent painting in Pontoise and Auvers were crucial to Cézanne's artistic development. Following Pissarro's example, he clarified his palette and used smaller brushes or, as in this work, special long, narrow and supple palette knives that enabled him to paint large or small masses of colour and to create a delicate or rough finish as he chose. Here, reflections, shadows and highlights are masterfully portrayed in a powerful composition.

Milk Bowl and Jug, 1873–7, oil on canvas, Bridgestone Museum of Art, Tokyo, Japan, 21 x 19cm (8 x 7in)

Delicate tints are placed in conjunction with stronger ones for a powerful impact reminiscent of the Spanish paintings that he had always admired. Cézanne painted this directly on to the canvas without a preparatory drawing, as was his method with many of his still lifes. The variegated brushstrokes anticipate the decomposition of forms that he began producing over the next couple of decades.

Plate with Grapes and Peach, c.1874–8, oil on canvas, Barnes Foundation, Philadelphia, PA, USA, 17 x 30cm (7 x 12in)

Toward the end of the 1870s, Cézanne wrote to Zola, "rather late, I have begun to see nature." This simple study comes alive with his new sunlit palette and broken brushwork that describes not only the surface textures of the fruit, china plate and wooden table, but also the solidity and weight of each object.

Bather with Outstretched Arms, c.1874–7, pencil on paper, Private Collection, 17 x 11cm (6 x 4in)

Among the most discussed, yet least explained works by Cézanne are his paintings from this study. He produced two in the late 1870s and early 1880s, and further oil sketches also relate to this drawing. The subject held his interest for about ten years, but the mystery of the image remains elusive. The boy is carefully constructed, but he seems more like a statue or sleepwalker than a bather.

A Painter at Work, 1874–5,
oil on canvas,
Private Collection,
24 x 34cm (9 x 13in)

With rich, buttery paint, Cézanne painted this in the year his work appeared in the first Impressionist exhibition. The bright palette and immediacy of brushwork are direct links with their work. It seems as if this was only ever intended to be a sketch and was never meant to become a final, finished composition. Uncharacteristically, he has made the figure fairly small in the centre of the work.

Bathers, 1873–7, oil on canvas, Metropolitan Museum of Art, New York, NY, USA, 38 x 46cm (15 x 18in)

The theme of nude figures in a landscape attracted Cézanne for a long time. This is one of his first paintings of the subject. Taking his time to balance the figures and the landscape, making both aspects equally important, he contradicted the fashionable, smooth and delicately realistic figure paintings of the period. The bright colours follow Impressionistic ideas of focusing on light.

Bathers, 1874–5,
oil on canvas, Musée
d'Orsay, Paris, France,
22 x 19cm (8 x 7in)

An admirer of classical and
Renaissance paintings of the
nude, Cézanne sought to
produce equally monumental
works in a more modern
idiom. Notoriously shy of
women, he did not use
female models, except
Hortense, so most of his
nude paintings are created
from his imagination.
This small canvas has
been painted with palette
knives, with a seemingly
spontaneous application
that was actually
carefully planned.

The Eternal Feminine,
c.1875–7, oil on canvas,
Getty Center,
Los Angeles, CA, USA,
42 x 53cm (17 x 21in)

On a small canvas, about
20 men gather in a semi-
circle around a naked
woman on a white sheet.
The men come from all
walks of life. Among others,
there are wrestlers, an artist,
a bishop with a mitre and
crosier, trumpeters, a
troubadour and a soldier.
The work is an allegory
of woman controlling the
world – by inciting desire in
every man.

The Hermitage, Pontoise,
c.1881, oil on canvas,
Von der Heydt-Museum,
Wuppertal, Germany,
47 x 56cm (19 x 22in)

Most of the landscapes that
Cézanne produced in the
1870s and 1880s combine
trees with houses, so he
could make the most of the
contrasts between geometric
forms and organic shapes.
Unlike the Impressionists, he
modified and re-arranged
what he saw before him for
the sake of the overall
design. Perspectives have
been altered and planes
tilted to give a strong sense
of structure.

Trees, c.1875–6, oil on
canvas, Private Collection,
56 x 74cm (22 x 29in)

With his instinctive
understanding of
composition, Cézanne
painted a variety of trees
in the grounds of the Jas
de Bouffan. He has taken
an interesting viewpoint,
directly across the grass, and
featured a triangular slice of
blue sky, like an arrow,
leading viewers' eyes directly
into the centre of the work.
His rich green hues radiate
both warm light and
cool shadows.

Bathers at Rest, c.1876–7, oil on canvas, Barnes Foundation, Philadelphia, PA, USA, 79 x 97cm (31 x 38in)

This large and ambitious impasto painting was exhibited in the third Impressionist exhibition of 1877. It was created after Cézanne had already produced two other versions, one in pen and ink and one in oil paint. The focal point is the central, standing figure, while the other three figures fit into the panoramic landscape dominated by Mont Sainte-Victoire in the background.

The Battle of Love, c.1880, oil on canvas, National Gallery of Art, Washington DC, USA, 38 x 46cm (15 x 18in)

The fine, parallel brush marks that have been built up in this painting were later described as 'constructive strokes.' They appeared first of all in his story-telling paintings, such as this and *The Eternal Feminine* (see page 131). A great deal has been read into this work that shows couples literally fighting for their love. It speaks volumes about Cézanne's attitude to women and romance.

Le Jas de Bouffan, c.1875–6,
oil on canvas,
Private Collection,
46 x 55cm (18 x 22in)

To try to combine what he was learning about Impressionism with his own desire for a more structured pictorial style, Cézanne continued to paint outdoors around the Jas de Bouffan. With a vivid palette and short, parallel, diagonal brushstrokes (that became more important and orderly through the decade), this appeared shockingly bright to viewers: "…the green makes one shudder…" wrote a critic.

Auvers, View of the Outskirts, c.1875–7, oil on canvas, Private Collection, 60 x 50cm (23 x 19in)

With his instinctive understanding of composition, Cézanne has captured a powerful scene that leads viewers' eyes through tall trees to the light-filled village beyond. His brushstrokes are emphatic, creating firm rhythms throughout the composition, hatched and broken, but always carefully planned – nothing has been left to chance, from the rich palette to the emphatic tones, to the angles of every mark.

Countryside around the River Oise, 1875, oil on canvas, Musée du Petit Palais, Geneva, Switzerland, 51 x 65cm (20 x 25in)

By the mid-1870s, Cézanne had developed what became known as his constructive brushstrokes. As in *The Battle of Love* (see page 133), these can be seen in this painting; structures of short marks in diagonal, horizontal or vertical angles, describing the movement or construction. The marks are parallel to each other in areas with an almost woven effect across his canvases, creating a coherent sense of texture and solidity.

Self-portrait (Portrait of the Artist with a Rose Background), c.1875, oil on canvas, Private Collection, Paris, 66 x 55cm (26 x 21in)

Throughout the 1870s, Cézanne regularly painted his self-portrait. It is difficult to work out the exact chronology of these, but his style is often a good indicator. In this work, his long, overlapping strokes of thick paint are not the constructive marks seen in the paintings on the previous two pages. It seems that for once, he was more intent on regarding the effects of passing time.

Flowers in a Blue Vase,
1873–5, oil on canvas,
State Hermitage Museum,
St Petersburg, Russia,
55 x 46cm (22 x 18 in)

Painted when he was staying
with Dr Gachet, Cézanne's
palette was becoming as
brilliant as the flowers that
Madame Gachet placed
about the house. Picking out
reflections and coloured
shadows, he also focused
on texture and form.
However, although the
subject could be described
as Impressionist, Cézanne
was looking at it in a
different light. He was not
aiming to capture a fleeting
impression but rather to
emphasize nature's
timelessness.

The Bathing Place, 1875–7,
oil on canvas,
Private Collection
19 x 27cm (7 x 10in)

This small work is in the
same style as many of
Cézanne's bather scenes,
particularly the *Three Bathers*
(see page 171) that was
owned by Matisse, who
wrote of it: "…I have owned
[the work] for 37 years.
I know this canvas rather
well, although I hope not
completely; it has provided
me with moral support in
critical moments in my
adventure as an artist; I have
drawn from it my faith and
my perseverance…"

The Sea at L'Estaque, 1876,
oil on canvas,
Private Collection,
42 x 59cm (16 x 23 in)

Painted for Victor Chocquet in June to July 1876, this is one of the few works by Cézanne that can be dated accurately. The landscape of L'Estaque was so bright and bold that he wrote enthusing about it to Pissarro and Guillemet, describing the strong contrasts of colours that bleached and flattened forms. He described the seemingly flat, colourful views as being "like a playing card."

Standing Nude, 1875–7,
oil on canvas,
Private Collection,
30 x 17cm (11 x 6in)

The fascination with nude figures in the landscape occasionally resulted in Cézanne painting a single figure. The vigorous brushwork and vibrant colours derive from his experiences with Pissarro, but the imaginary figure (he rarely depicted nudes directly from life) and the observed setting are completely unique to him. This male figure appears to be singing as he dries his back.

Overturned Basket of Fruit,
c.1877, oil on canvas,
Art Gallery and Museum,
Glasgow, Scotland,
16 x 32cm (6 x 13in)

In accordance with many of Cézanne's still lifes of this time, this composition of a basket of fruit overturned and the contents spilling out, is simple but unconventional. Placed at an angle and boldly taking up most of the canvas, the fruit is depicted in a broad range of colours and tones. These still lifes of fruit appealed, surprisingly, to Degas, who bought several of them.

Compotier and Plate of
Biscuits, c.1877,
oil on canvas, Private
Collection, Japan,
54 x 64cm (21 x 25in)

The wallpaper in this work is distinctive and appears in several works by Cézanne around this time. It is believed to be the wallpaper that was on the walls of an apartment he occupied sporadically during 1877, 1878 and 1879, at 67 rue l'Ouest in Paris. The painting also features his constructive brushstrokes. They are applied in the same descriptive manner across the canvas and are definite, defined, compact and methodical.

Still Life with a Soup Tureen, 1877, oil on canvas, Musée d'Orsay, Paris, France, 65 x 83cm (25 x 32in)

A landscape by Pissarro hangs on the wall behind this still life arrangement, indicating that this was painted in Pissarro's house in Pontoise. The soft brushwork and vivid colours convey the play of light on the forms of each object, building up the impression of solidity without shadows or atmospheric perspective. Cézanne was also starting to paint objects from several viewpoints at once.

*Pears on a Chair, c.*1879–80, oil on canvas, Barnes Foundation, Philadelphia, PA, USA, 20 x 37cm (8 x 15in)

The parallel slanting brushstrokes create contrast within the entire surface pattern across the canvas. The red pear has broadly applied brushwork, the upright pear has more individual brushstrokes and the brushwork on the chair is even more contrasting, with definite colours, shapes and tones that form patterns of small hatchings. This produces an impression of flatness, but volume and solidity are created through accentuated dark contour lines.

Tiger, after Barye, c.1876–7,
oil on canvas,
Private Collection,
29 x 37cm (11 x 14in)

Cézanne painted this small
work after Antoine-Louis
Barye (1796–1875). Barye
was known for his animal
sculptures and Cézanne

admired one of his
lithographs of a tiger. It is an
unusual subject for Cézanne
and not something that he
repeated. The work is richly
painted with a brush loaded
with pigment, and the
impasto finish in subtle and
soft colours creates texture
– again, unusual for Cézanne.

Self-portrait, c.1877–80, oil
on canvas, Musée d'Orsay,
Paris, France,
26 x 15cm (10 x 6in)

Cézanne drew or painted
himself many times, usually
trying to depict physical
reality rather than emotional
expression. This work once
belonged to Pissarro. It was

painted around the time
that Cézanne's father found
out about his mistress
and son, so perhaps
naturally, he looks older
in this than in many later
self-portraits. In contrast
with his clandestine
relationship, his youngest
sister, Rose, was engaged
to a lawyer.

Cup, Glass and Fruit, 1877,
oil on canvas,
Private Collection,
34 x 46cm (13 x 18in)

As with all Cézanne's still
lifes, there is a relationship
between each object and
the negative spaces around

them. He saw painting as a
synthesis of line and colour.
"When colour is at its
richest, form is at its fullest,"
he remarked. To this end, he
examined the fall of light on
everything so he could
endow it with the maximum
sensory effect as a painting.

Still Life with Open Drawer,
1877–9, oil on canvas,
Private Collection,
33 x 47cm (13 x 18in)

This was among the still lifes
to which Georges Rivière
referred when he defended
Cézanne after the third
unsuccessful Impressionist
exhibition in Paris in 1877.
"…His canvases exude the
calmness and heroic serenity
of ancient terracotta
ceramics and decoration
[…] His still lifes are so
beautiful and so precise in
the harmony of their tones.
There is a sort of solemn
truth about them."

The Sea at L'Estaque, 1878, oil on canvas, Musée Picasso, Paris, France, 73 x 92cm (28 x 36in)

A horizontal path runs along the bottom of this canvas, while trees grow up to frame the view between. The branches act like curtains on a stage, framing the town below, and as usual, Cézanne's colours express all. Red roofs contrast with green vegetation, curving organic forms contrast with geometric buildings, while the chimney adds depth to the scene, rising high above the buildings and in front of the aquamarine sea.

Still Life with Apples, 1878, oil on canvas, Private Collection, 18 x 38cm (7 x 15in)

Along with the more well-known still lifes of apples with other objects, Cézanne sometimes painted only isolated fruit. This can be viewed as a study for a more ambitious painting. Nevertheless, some of these studies, made at close range, have proved to be among his most admired works. With precision and deftness using small brushes, he has painted an incredible variety and intensity of colour and tone.

The Bay of L'Estaque,
*c.*1878–82, pencil,
watercolour and gouache
on pale yellow
paper, Kunsthaus,
Zürich, Switzerland,
29 x 46cm (11 x 18in)

Using the transparency of
watercolour with touches
of opaque gouache, Cézanne
blended a limited palette of
colours to achieve a brilliant
study of the sparkling bay.
Here, complementary
colours are juxtaposed to
invigorate the entire
composition; ultramarine is
echoed in the greenery and
red ochre appears in the
roofs, earth and shadows.

Five Bathers, 1877–8, oil on
canvas, Musée Picasso,
Paris, France, 46 x 56cm
(18 x 22in)

In the late 1870s and early
1880s, Cézanne painted
several small canvases of
female bathers in an almost
square format. Each is
created with rich colours,
particularly the emerald and
chartreuse greens he often
used, and each features his
constructive parallel and
diagonal brushstrokes.
Picasso bought this work in
the late 1950s and Matisse
bought another of a similar
subject and format.

L'Estaque, Evening Effect, c.1878, oil on canvas, Musée du Louvre, Paris, France, 44 x 60cm (17 x 24in)

The spectacular panoramas and dazzling colours of L'Estaque refreshed and invigorated Cézanne. In comparison with his Impressionist work of recent years, his canvases became bold and intensely coloured. This dramatic composition half taken up with the rocky headland is one of the few canvases he painted there level with the sea; most of his other works of the location are from a raised perspective.

The Chaîne de l'Étoile with the Pilon du Roi, c.1878–9, oil on canvas, Kelvingrove, Art Gallery and Museum, Glasgow, Scotland, 49 x 59cm (19 x 23in)

Demonstrating his skills as a natural colourist, Cézanne painted this when all around him his friends were beginning to experience recognition and he was still being ridiculed. Seemingly unflustered and relaxed, he painted this view of the Chaine de l'Etoile, which is a small mountain range located north of Marseilles. He captured its elegance and colours in shades of orange, gold, violet, green, pink and blue.

The Pool at the Jas de Bouffan, 1878, oil on canvas, Private Collection, 47 x 56cm (18 x 22in)

On his return to Aix from L'Estaque early in 1878, Cézanne painted some more austere compositions than he had been producing of late. In this work, empty spaces appear in several places, while the tree in the centre with its vertical reflection becomes the focal point. Several rectangular shapes are repeated, as Cézanne distilled the original image, stripping it to essentials with nothing superfluous. It heralds abstractions of the mid-20th century.

Landscape near Paris, c.1876, oil on canvas, National Gallery of Art, Washington, DC, USA, 50 x 60cm (20 x 23in)

With his lighter, Impressionist-inspired palette, Cézanne, unlike his contemporaries, largely ignored settings of urban life in favour of the countryside. This was about as close as he would go to painting an outdoor Parisian scene. In 1876, he had refused to exhibit with the Impressionists again, choosing instead to work on his independent vision. He never rejected his public identity as an Impressionist, but the artists all knew from the outset that he was pursuing a different path.

Portrait of the Artist's Wife, 1878, oil on canvas, Nationalmuseum, Stockholm, Sweden, 73 x 56cm (29 x 22in)

This is one of the rare occasions in which Cézanne captured Hortense in a relaxed moment. With her light-blue outfit contrasting with her usual dark clothes, this is a more human view of his future wife (they married in 1886). The composition almost thrusts her at viewers and yet seemingly without any encroachment upon her concentration. The mix of primary colours is not jarring and she looks calm.

The Pool at the Jas de Bouffan, c.1878–9, oil on canvas, Albright-Knox Art Gallery, New York, NY, USA, 92 x 80cm (36 x 31in)

Once again turning to his home and the surroundings he knew and loved so well, Cézanne has made a feature of parallels, contrasts of straight and curving lines and of verdant greens, cool blues and golds. The brushstrokes show Pissarro's influence once again. The fact that he was so familiar with the subject meant that he could investigate beyond the superficial appearance.

Still Life with a Dessert, c.1877–9, oil on canvas, Philadelphia Museum of Art, PA, USA, 59 x 73cm (23 x 29in)

Set against an ochre coloured background are a cut-glass carafe, glass and fruit on an elegant sideboard. The light is sharp, the colours bright and the tones are even and calm. By selecting a variety of inanimate objects, Cézanne's explorations intensified into the similarities and differences in colour and forms of each of the objects and of the negative spaces around and between them.

Still Life with Apples and a Glass of Wine, 1877–9, oil on canvas, Philadelphia Museum of Art, PA, USA, 27 x 33cm (11 x 13in)

Apples from Provence were a strong symbol of Aix. By juxtaposing other objects and colours, he was examining complex relationships as well as objects' inherent structures. Captured as if by chance, he actually spent a lot of time arranging the objects and then even more time studying them from different angles before painting them.

Île de France, c.1879, oil on canvas, Private Collection, 46 x 56cm (18 x 22in)

Between March and April 1879, Cézanne was in Paris and worked closely with Guillaumin. The pair had been friends since Cézanne's arrival in Paris and at the Atelier Suisse and Cézanne often rented a studio near Guillaumin. During the 1860s and 1870s, they often painted together, sometimes on expeditions to the outskirts of Paris. This was painted in the Île de France, a region to the north-east of Paris.

Avenue in the Park of Chantilly, c.1879, oil on canvas, Göteborgs Konstmuseum, Sweden, 74 x 61cm (29 x 24in)

This painting was bought by Gauguin from Père Tanguy during the summer of 1883, plus another work, *Mountains in Provence*. He paid 120 francs for the pair. The brushstrokes are mostly diagonally slanted but so loosely assembled that the grey priming of the canvas can be seen clearly between the strokes. Cézanne worked with traditional one-point perspective, something he was soon to abandon.

Bottom of the Ravine, 1879, oil on canvas, Museum of Fine Arts, Houston, TX, USA, 73 x 54cm (28 x 21in)

Painted not far from Aix, Cézanne constructed this scene with areas of dabbed colour, treating each element with equal weight, which results in a balance of forms and colours. He said, "There are two things in painting: vision and mind, and they should work in unison. As a painter, one must try to develop them harmoniously: vision, by looking at nature; mind, by ruling one's senses logically, thus providing the means of expression."

*Plums and Pears, c.*1879, oil on canvas, Barnes Foundation, Philadelphia, PA, USA, 20 x 36cm (8 x 14in)

This study of fruit and a jar demonstrates Cézanne's investigations into geometric volumes in space. With patches of colour placed equally to depict the objects, spaces between them and the wallpaper background, he challenges viewers' perception of visual space. The paint marks appear roughly applied, because they were initial layers – the work is unfinished.

Jalais Hill, Pontoise, 1879–81,
oil on canvas,
Private Collection,
60 x 76cm (23 x 30in)

This view of Jalais Hill near
Pontoise is characterized by
a powerful composition,
strong brushstrokes and
broad, flat areas of colour –
all owing much to the work
of Courbet and Corot as
well as to Pissarro, who
painted the same subject
alongside Cézanne at
this time. For once, Zola
admired this work
and believed that
Cézanne was at last
getting somewhere
with his ambition.

Landscape, Aix-en-Provence,
1879, oil on canvas,
Private Collection,
46 x 55cm (18 x 21in)

"I wanted to make
Impressionism solid and
durable, like the art of the
museums," Cézanne declared
to Maurice Denis near the
end of his life. Here can
still be seen the vestiges
of his Impressionistic
experimentations in a
sketchy rendition of the
countryside in Aix. Yet his
parallel brushstrokes still
reveal his interest in making
the motif more solid and
deliberately rendered.

The Bridge at Maincy, c.1879,
oil on canvas, Musée
d'Orsay, Paris, France,
59 x 73cm (23 x 29in)

In this intensely coloured
work, painted when he was
staying at Melun, Cézanne's
feathered Impressionistic
brushstrokes have gone
and are replaced with
the constructive marks he
developed for the rest of his
life. With these firm, parallel
marks, he conveyed the way
light travels through the
scene, capturing colourfully
ordered reflections and a
strong sense of place with
a patterned, woven effect.

Still Life with Fruit, c.1879,
oil on canvas, State
Hermitage Museum,
St Petersburg, Russia,
45 x 55cm (17 x 22in)

Ordinary objects were
extremely important to
Cézanne. Through them, he
could explore shape, form,
colour, tone and his personal
perceptions. By their
solidity and stability, he
could carefully study and
draw each element that
concerned him. He placed
the objects carefully, and
tried to express permanence
and to show the
completeness of the objects,
by portraying them from
different angles at once.

Still Life, c.1879–80, oil on canvas, Private Collection, 50 x 61cm (19 x 24in)

Cézanne told Bernard that the painter "gives a new interest to…nature" and "renders as a painter that which has not yet been painted." His own uniqueness developed through his handling of paint and colour, which can be seen clearly here. All the colours, applied with his small dashes and layered carefully, react with each other. Warm colours advance and cool colours recede, so they produce effects of relief and recession.

Jug, Fruit, Cloth and Glass, c.1879, oil on canvas, Musée de l'Orangerie, Paris, France, 60 x 73cm (23 x 28in)

Taking a high viewpoint, Cézanne placed objects on a sideboard against the wallpaper he often used as the background for his works. This ochre-coloured, diamond-patterned paper adds to the complex play of diagonals, which are countered by the rounded shapes of the fruit, curves of the napkin and straight lines of the sideboard, knife and jug. The white curve of the napkin is used to link the individual objects together.

Milk Jar and Lemon, c.1879,
oil on canvas, Private
Collection, Switzerland,
22 x 44cm (9 x 17in)

The rough-hewn shapes that Cézanne created in several of his still lifes at the end of the 1870s resemble his landscapes featuring Mont Sainte-Victoire. In this work, his layered paint marks are reminiscent of his treatment of those towering vistas. He continued to avoid traditional perspective and to paint objects from different angles in order to show the entirety of an object and not just a snapshot view.

Still Life with Fruit, 1879–80,
oil on canvas,
Private Collection,
46 x 55cm (18 x 21in)

Breaking up the horizontal bands in the background with rounded forms in the foreground, Cézanne established a calm, balanced composition. This is further enhanced with his tonal gradations, from the deepest to the lightest and the combinations of dark, delicate, sombre and bright colours. His brushwork creates dynamism between every element on the canvas and fuses everything together, creating the coherence he believed was imperative.

Leaving on the Water,
1879–82, oil on canvas,
Private Collection,
26 x 34cm (10 x 13in)

From April 1879 to March 1880, Cézanne lived in Melun with Hortense and Paul. Close to the River Seine and about 50km (30 miles) to the south-east of Paris, Melun was a colourful, picturesque and inspiring place. Since his early days of Delacroix-inspired romantic paintings, Cézanne had not painted such an active scene and this is fairly uncharacteristic of the time, but continues to assert his powerful compositional skills.

Portrait of Victor Chocquet,
1877–80, oil on canvas,
Columbus Museum
of Art, OH, USA,
46 x 38cm (18 x 15in)

From his wife's inheritance, Chocquet began collecting art, first by his hero Delacroix, followed by Courbet and then Renoir.

He became the first real collector of Cézanne's art, buying 33 paintings. Cézanne soon began this first portrait of Chocquet. When Degas saw the work in progress, he commented: "The portrait of a madman made by a madman." Later, Degas became an avid admirer of Cézanne's work.

Madame Cézanne in the
Garden, **1879–80, oil on canvas, Musée de l'Orangerie, Paris, France, 88 x 66cm (34 x 26in)**

Hortense was a constant and patient model, but she never fully grasped the importance of Cézanne's work and achievements. Although she was reputed to love fashion, she often appears in his works dressed rather severely, and her lack of intellect or meaningfu conversation irritated his Impressionist friends, who nicknamed her 'The Ball' after the shape of her head. In this unfinished work, her expression seems to convey that she was posing reluctantly.

Village Road, c.1879–82,
oil on canvas,
Private Collection,
54 x 45cm (21 x 17in)

Using the device of a curving road as a central void, receding from viewers, Cézanne demonstrated all he had learned from Pissarro. He was still aiming to create an inherently balanced and organized harmony within his landscapes, but he often included his friend's theories at this time, such as this prospect of a distant village framed by a wall on both sides and trees on the left.

Apples and Biscuits, 1879–82, oil on canvas, Musée de l'Orangerie, Paris, France, 45 x 55cm (17 x 21in)

One of seven still lifes of apples and other simple objects placed on a wooden storage chest in front of a blue-grey wallpaper decorated with a delicate floral pattern, this is about the simplest composition of them all. Only one red apple rises above the horizon of the wooden chest, the rest lie scattered (albeit carefully placed) and shown by the tilt of the chest.

The Bath, 1879–82, oil on canvas, Staatsgalerie, Stuttgart, Germany, 33 x 22cm (13 x 8in)

Less defined than several other bather paintings, this long thin canvas shows three women washing in the open air. Returning to sketchier, more varied brushwork, using a variety of colours across the canvas and refraining from too many layers, Cézanne, after several years, has reverted to a more Impressionistic style once again.

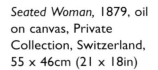

Seated Woman, 1879, oil on canvas, Private Collection, Switzerland, 55 x 46cm (21 x 18in)

This unidentified woman has been portrayed in a similar manner to the portraits Cézanne rendered of Hortense. Her gaze, although not shown in detail, is slightly confrontational and her hands are unfinished, but Cézanne's application of paint is confident and descriptive, uniting the blouse and the background with similar colours and brushwork, while the table top in the bottom left slopes towards viewers.

Landscape in Provence, 1880, pencil, watercolour and gouache on paper, Kunsthaus, Zürich, Switzerland, 35 x 50cm (14 x 20in)

By the end of the 1870s, Cézanne had established his resolve to go in a different direction to the Impressionists. He respected what they were doing but placed no trust in the idea of superficial impressions. For him it was a question of sincerity – by painting several views at once, he felt he was being more truthful in what he was painting. Using pencil, watercolour and gouache, he was able to investigate colour differently.

Self-portrait, 1880, oil on canvas, National Gallery, London, UK, 33 x 26cm (13 x 10in)

Once again the ochre coloured latticed wallpaper is evident, this time behind the artist himself. His calm, contemplative expression does not detract from the relationships between the shapes and forms surrounding his head. Diamond shapes are repeated within his face, jacket, beard, nose and eyes, in a cohesive effort to connect the subject with the background.

Château de Médan, 1880, oil on canvas, Burrell Collection, Glasgow, Scotland, 59 x 72cm (23 x 28in)

More geometric accents began appearing in Cézanne's landscapes by the 1880s. By reinforcing vertical and horizontal lines, he created networks of objects within several scenes. This is one that he painted from an island in the Seine during a summer visit to Zola. The Château de Médan can be seen more clearly than in his earlier watercolours of it, at the right-hand side with other buildings in clear contrast with the surrounding trees.

Landscape in Provence, 1880, watercolour, Museum of Fine Arts, Budapest, Hungary, 31 x 48cm (12 x 19in)

The precision of Cézanne's drawing combines here with his loose touches of watercolour, which, in comparison to thick oil pigment, was used for sketches for his main works. Here he has built up volumes with free and translucent touches of watercolour. His watercolours were not intended for exhibition, but for experiments with colour.

Château de Médan, 1880, pencil, watercolour and gouache on paper, Kunsthaus, Zürich, Switzerland, 31 x 47cm (12 x 19in)

While Cézanne was frequently visiting Zola at his country house in Médan, he painted this study of the landscape in a mix of transparent watercolour and opaque gouache. The three horizontal bands from the bank of the river accentuate stability, while the vertical trees create an almost grid-like arrangement across the entire image. Predominantly green, there are some brilliant touches of cobalt blue between the trees.

Self-portrait, 1880, oil on canvas, Neue Pinakothek, Munich, Germany, 56 x 46cm (22 x 18in)

This shows a new level of assurance that Cézanne had attained with his painting. The portrait is built up with layered short strokes in a palette of browns, ochre and reds, with underlying cool colours. The choice of this cotton plasterer's hat is a little odd, but not unlike one that Chardin wears in a similar self-portrait.

Flowers in a Blue Vase,
c.1886, oil on canvas,
Musée de l'Orangerie,
Paris, France,
37 x 28cm (14 x 11in)

As one of the first avant-garde artists to move beyond a concern with atmospheric effects to a new emphasis on geometric structure in painting, Cézanne tried different types of strokes to express texture and solidity. Here, impasto paint in vigorous strokes deliberately accentuates the contrasting colours. Using a distinct palette and an intense range of tones, this is a particularly modern-looking work.

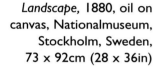

Landscape, 1880, oil on canvas, Nationalmuseum, Stockholm, Sweden, 73 x 92cm (28 x 36in)

"In order to paint a landscape well, I first need to discover the geological foundations…I mentally sketch out the rocky skeleton." This was Cézanne's aim and he explored it in different ways with every work that he produced. He wanted to portray nature without using lines, only colour patches, and so he did not include lines in his oil paintings; colour did the job of showing contour and form.

*Still Life with Flowers in an Olive Jar, c.*1880, oil on canvas, Philadelphia Museum of Art, PA, USA, 46 x 34cm (18 x 13in)

The olive jar is recognizable from other still lifes and has been used to create a particularly strong composition, with emphasis on tonal contrasts and diagonal lines drawing viewers' eyes into and around the image. He explained his working method to Joachim Gasquet: "…You must understand that I work on the whole canvas, on everything at once… our art must render the thrill of [nature's] permanence along with her elements."

Auvers-sur-Oise, 1879–82, oil on canvas, Ashmolean Museum, Oxford, UK (stolen 31 December 1999), 45 x 54cm (17 x 21in)

Pitching his easel before the lush valley and picturesque village of Auvers as he had done several times before, Cézanne continued to apply the formula he had learned from Pissarro, searching for the infinite variety of contrasts between lights and darks. But by the beginning of the 1880s, his 'transitional phase' had begun, whereby he began 'sculpting' his brush marks to emphasize the structural framework of all he perceived.

Viaduct at L'Estaque, 1882, oil on canvas, Allen Memorial Art Museum, Oberlin College, OH, USA, 47 x 56cm (19 x 22in)

Painted when Renoir was visiting him at L'Estaque, Cézanne has emphasized the density and rugged nature of the landscape in his usual way by creating a bold composition with the massive, impenetrable rock taking up most of the canvas. The subtle colour variations and the energetic brushwork, no longer inflexible or angled specifically, lead the eye from the foreground trees to the distant crags against the sky.

*Countryside, c.*1881, oil on canvas, Private Collection, 46 x 55cm (18 x 22in)

Probably produced on one of Cézanne's painting trips in Pontoise when he went out with Pissarro and Gauguin, this seems to be another attempt at the Impressionism he had left behind, perhaps because being in Pontoise reminded him of his earlier time there with Pissarro. Using a slightly different colour palette, the landscape is more about the surface view, although he was still considering structure and how to convey it.

The Uphill Road, 1881, oil on canvas, National Gallery of Victoria, Melbourne, Australia, 59 x 71cm (23 x 28in)

Painted when he was staying with Pissarro at Pontoise, Cézanne chose this angle so he could explore the contrasts and connections between the geometric buildings and the undulating, organic landscape. His style here, with thin layers of paint, varied brushwork and a light palette, shows aspects of Impressionism and Pissarro's influence as well as his later constructive approach. The work was never finished.

SERENITY AND STRENGTH

As his style developed, all Cézanne had learned from the old masters and from Pissarro amalgamated in his palette and his constructional brushwork. Paintings in each genre, landscape, still life and portraits, became varied and more accomplished. Although he continued to make much of contrast, this became subtler than in his early works – he no longer merely used blacks and whites, but incorporated innumerable hues and tonal varieties. He still ranged between acute self-doubt (even at 50 he wrote that "the many studies to which I have dedicated myself have given me only negative results") and a conviction that what he was doing was right and that he could achieve something that was unique and significant.

Above: Female Nude on a Sofa*, oil on canvas, Van der Heydt Museum, Wuppertal, Germany, 43 x 61cm (17 x 24in).*
Left: Self-portrait with a Bowler Hat, *1883–5, oil on canvas, Private Collection, 41 x 34cm (16 x 13in).*

View of Mount Mareseilleveyre and the Isle of Maire, c.1882–5, oil on canvas, Private Collection, 62 x 51cm (24 x 20in)

In his paintings of the 1880s, directional brushstrokes and patterns of warm and cool colours helped Cézanne to organize his visual sensations. In similar compositions to his earlier views of L'Estaque, he reveals his interest in bold colours and exploration of structure in everything, from solid trees and rocks to the sea, distant mountains and the sky. Transitory effects of light and atmosphere are included, but only up to a point.

Farmhouse in Normandy, 1882, oil on canvas, Private Collection, 50 x 66cm (20 x 26in)

Many of Cézanne's landscapes are similar in their compositions. He frequently included specific elements such as trees, branches, a small clearing or an avenue of trees. In this work, the dense green abundance of the foliage resembles several other landscapes of the time, including *The Bridge at Maincy* and *Poplars,* for example. Unlike their close hatched marks, though, this features soft golden light filtering through the slightly out-of-focus scene.

Homestead in Normandy-Hattenville, 1882, oil on canvas, Private Collection, 50 x 65cm (19 x 25in)

In March 1882, Victor Chocquet's mother-in-law died. Chocquet's wife was the sole heir; she inherited a substantial fortune and her mother's farm in Normandy near the village of Hattenville. Chocquet was then enabled to give up his job and retire to the country. He invited Cézanne to stay and paint in the grounds of the farm and this is one of the works he produced there.

Mont Sainte-Victoire and the Viaduct of the Arc River, c.1882–5, oil on canvas, Metropolitan Museum of Art, New York, NY, USA, 65 x 82cm (26 x 32in)

To capture this view, Cézanne stood at the top of a hill just behind Bellevue, where his sister Rose Conil and her husband lived. This vast panoramic view of the Arc river valley and its simple buildings and patchwork of fields, leading up to his favourite motif, is divided by a tall, thin tree that also serves to stitch the image together and draw viewers' eyes in and around.

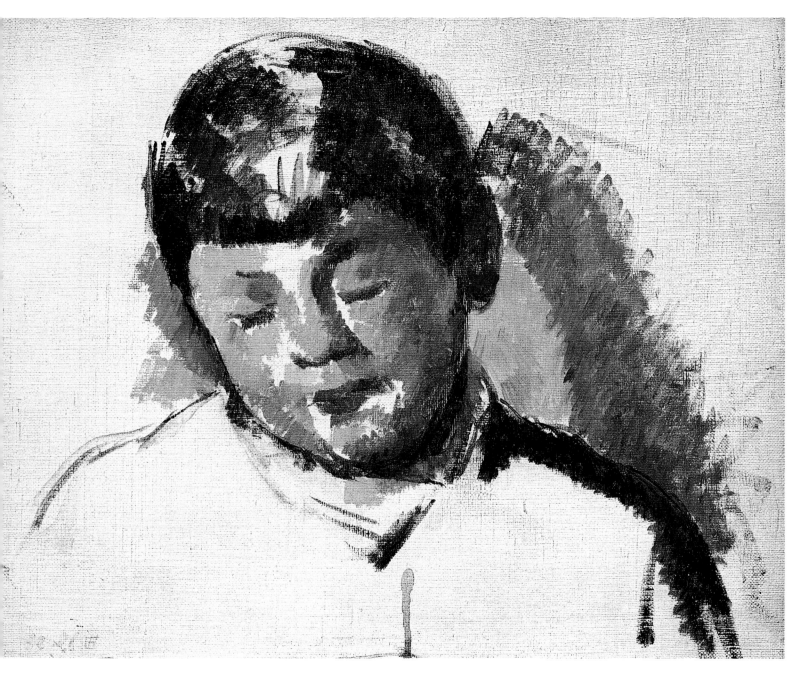

Paul Cézanne, Son of the Artist, 1882, oil on canvas, Wadsworth Atheneum, Hartford, CT, USA, 28 x 32cm (11 x 13in)

Young Paul became a probably reluctant, but frequent sitter for his father, especially as he grew up. This sketch was made when he was about ten and was one of many that the proud father made to chart his son's development. Cézanne captured him in many different poses, such as sleeping, reading or drawing and sometimes smiling mischievously, knowing that he could get his doting father to agree to almost anything.

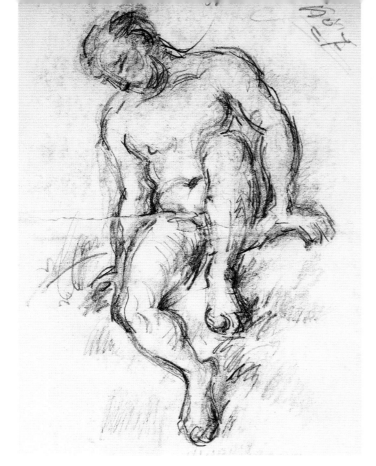

Seated Male Bather, 1882, pencil on paper, Philadelphia Museum of Art, PA, USA, 22 x 13cm (9 x 5in)

Although 1882 was the year that Cézanne achieved his aim of exhibiting at the Salon, reality turned out to be a very different experience from the one that he had imagined. He spent a great deal of time in the Louvre, sketching from sculpture he admired – and waiting for his life to change as a result of exhibiting at the Salon. When nothing happened, he returned to Aix via Médan and Zola.

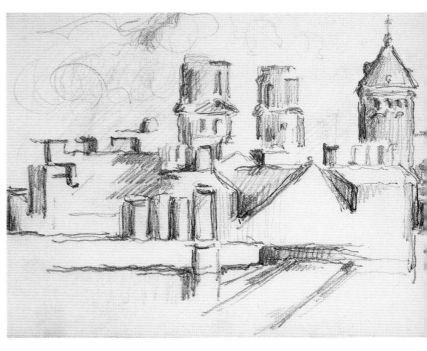

View of Paris, 1882, pencil on paper, Philadelphia Museum of Art, PA, USA, 12 x 18cm (5 x 7in)

Although drawing and painting had not come easily to Cézanne when he was younger, by this point in his career, his drawings were deft and assured. Although in his paintings he depicted objects from different angles simultaneously in order to show the entire structure, in his drawings, he adhered to traditional conventions of linear perspective.

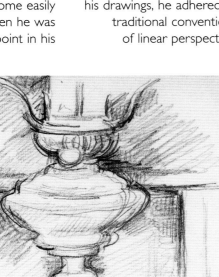

Kerosene Lamp and Books, 1882, pencil on paper, Philadelphia Museum of Art, PA, USA, 19 x 12cm (7 x 4in)

With a skilful hand, Cézanne has sketched the essentials of this kerosene lamp and even in a small study has paid attention to the essentials of composition. He made the most of whatever he portrayed, never relegating anything to mediocrity, and this modest object has become monumental and powerful, made important through its size and position on the paper, captured with a few strokes of the pencil.

*The Aqueduct and Canal at Verdun, c.*1883, oil on canvas, Private Collection, Switzerland. 59 x 73cm (23 x 28in)

Verdun lies to the north of Aix and was one of Cézanne and Zola's favourite childhood places. While the nimble brushwork tends to flatten the image, it also helps to create a sense of the distances that can be glimpsed through the bushes and trees. Another of Cézanne's compositional methods, this 'looking through' leads viewers' eyes beyond the foliage to the aqueduct and patterns of fields and houses.

*Portrait of Paul Cézanne Junior, c.*1885, oil on canvas, Jan Krugier & Marie-Anne Krugier-Poniatowski Collection, Geneva, Switzerland, 26 x 20cm (10 x 8in)

Cézanne's quickly sketched images of Paul as he grew up are evidence of the love the father held for his son; for no one else would he rush a painting. Even unfinished, this sensitive portrait clearly shows Paul's cheeky attitude to his father and Cézanne has captured him grinning impishly, a facial expression he rarely portrayed in his portraits.

Three Bathers, 1879–82, oil on canvas, Musée du Petit Palais de la Ville de Paris, Paris, France, 52 x 55cm (20 x 21in)

For over 30 years, this painting belonged to Matisse and inevitably has been regarded as a major influence in the history of 20th-century art. This is an excerpt of a letter from Matisse to the Petit Palais about it: "…this picture is of the first importance in Cézanne's oeuvre, for it is the very dense and very complete realization of a composition much studied by him…"

Bathers, 1883–5, oil on canvas, Private Collection, 36 x 45cm (14 x 18in)

In his mid-40s, Cézanne continued to paint his lively and strong bather paintings, with figures held in place by oblique parallel brushstrokes and bright, fresh colours in the landscape. Unlike his earlier paintings of bathers, these figures appear to be communicating with each other, suggesting that after several years, Cézanne was trying to reintroduce narrative into his work, even though the figures remain anonymous and indeterminate.

Mont Sainte-Victoire, c.1882–5, oil on canvas, Pushkin State Museum of Fine Arts, Moscow, Russia, 58 x 72cm (22 x 28in)

By the end of 1882, Cézanne's technique was changing again. It continued to evolve throughout his life, but at this point, despite the lack of recognition, he seemed to be more assured about his individual path. This work includes Mont Sainte-Victoire, but it is merely part of the scene, not the most important part of it, and the focus is more on the shape of his brushwork.

Still Life with a Peach and Two Green Pears, 1883–7, oil on canvas, Private Collection, 37 x 45cm (15 x 18in)

With oblique brush marks following the forms and a brilliant but restricted palette, Cézanne has fully explored his methods of showing objects in two dimensions from several angles simultaneously. To Bernard he explained h s method of modelling w th colour: "The secret of drawing and modelling [is in] contrasts and relationships of colours"; and to Der is he said: "Colour has to express all the breaks in depth."

Still Life on a Table, 1883–7, oil on canvas, Neue Pinakothek, Munich, Germany, 71 x 90cm (28 x 35in)

Cézanne painted this same still life twice at about the same time, which was uncharacteristic. He often painted the same objects, but he usually arranged them differently. This composition interested him: curved and straight lines, dark and light contrasts, a mix of manmade and natural forms – all adding to the challenge of perception and portrayal.

Girl with a Birdcage,
c.1885, oil on canvas,
Barnes Foundation,
Philadelphia, PA, USA,
45 x 37cm (17x 15in)

Although this work might seem to be incongruous with the type of work Cézanne was producing at the time, the use of overlapping planes makes it consistent with his methods, even if the final appearance is not familiar. The stiff, unnatural posture of the girl was not his main concern; he was intent on exploring solid forms and relationships between structures.

Madame Cézanne with Loosened Hair, 1883–5, oil on canvas, Private Collection, 62 x 51cm (24 x 20in)

Hortense rarely sat for Cézanne in anything other than fashionable attire with groomed hair. In October 1906, when summoned to his deathbed, she even stopped at her dressmaker's on the way and arrived too late, so this image with her hair unbound is unusual and reveals a more relaxed moment – also indicated by his animated, fluid brushstrokes. He usually painted her simply in terms of formal elements, like a still life.

*Winter Landscape, c.1885,
oil on canvas,
Private Collection,
61 x 73cm (24 x 28in)*

Largely unconcerned about
new approaches that other
painters were instigating,
Cézanne's development of
the parallel brushstroke
as a means for creating an
orderly portrayal of forms
was unique and original.
He was aware of its novelty
and power and fiercely
protective of it. In this
unfinished work, his
method can be seen from
its earliest stages.

Médan Château and Village,
1885, oil on canvas,
Art Focus Gallery,
Zürich, Switzerland,
81 x 65cm (32 x 26in)

Set in horizontal bands of
green trees and terracotta
rooftops, this unfinished
work reveals Cézanne's
working method. He
sketched the entire
landscape first in a thin
wash and then began
applying densely packed
directional marks in ranges
of rich colours. One of the
differences between him
and the Impressionists
was that his application of
these parallel, directional
marks was a method
of painting and not a
sensory experience.

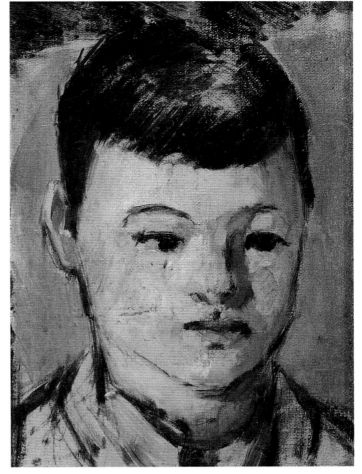

Paul Cézanne, the Artist's Son, 1884–6, oil on canvas, Von der Heydt-Museum, Wuppertal, Germany, 20 x 12cm (8 x 5in)

Although this portrait has been dated when Paul was aged twelve to fourteen, he looks about nine or ten years old and certainly younger than the portrait on page 170, which is dated 1885. As Cézanne rarely dated his works, this is a common problem. Unlike the previous portrait of Hortense and the majority of Cézanne's paintings, this work reveals evidence of the sitter's personality, captured by a doting father.

Self-portrait with Palette, 1884–7, oil on canvas, E. G. Bührle Collection, Zürich, Switzerland, 93 x 73cm (37 x 28in)

This is the only one of Cézanne's self-portraits that shows more than his head and shoulders and the only one that shows him as an artist at work. Standing in front of his easel, he holds his palette, a rectangle, parallel to the bottom and left edge of the canvas. Patches of colour and tone have been built up with blues, golds and greens to create an image that portrays a sense of isolation.

Landscape in the Midi,
c.1885–7, oil on canvas,
Private Collection,
63 x 94cm (24 x 37in)

For most of 1885, Cézanne was in Aix or L'Estaque, embarking on a fairly settled period of painting. With a light touch and thin paint, Cézanne has built up this image almost like a watercolour. The manner in which he built up the structure of the landscape, using variegated brush marks, can be seen quite clearly here in the initial stages of the painting – every work he undertook went through many stages as he developed the image he was aiming for.

Landscape with Poplars,
1885–7, oil on canvas,
National Gallery,
London, UK,
71 x 58cm (28 x 22in)

This is probably one of five landscapes that Cézanne painted almost simultaneously as he experimented with repeated patterns of parallel diagonal and vertical brushstrokes. Although his aim was always to make something durable out of his representations and he was still looking for ways to illustrate the essence of what he saw, the brushstrokes here suggest shimmering sunlight illuminating the various textures of the foliage.

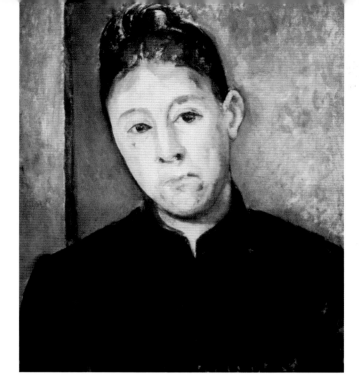

Madame Cézanne, 1885–6, oil on canvas, Musée d'Orsay, Paris, France, 46 x 38cm (18 x 15in)

Cézanne did not understand women and Hortense did not understand his art, but in 1886, they were married and for a while, she continued to be his main model. Her remote, inscrutable look that did not reveal her feelings has been replaced by a miserable expression and her eyes for once are fixed on the viewer. Cézanne did not intend to create an emotional work, but for once he allowed some subjectivity to penetrate.

Hillside Landscape near Médan, c.1885, oil on canvas, Private Collection, 65 x 81cm (25 x 31in)

In almost scribbled, directional brush marks, Cézanne has described texture in his initial applications of paint. With his multitude of greens, he has started to build up the landscape using horizontal bands in faceted and delicate chromatics. Perhaps because the work is unfinished, or because this was a method he was experimenting with, the application appears lighter in touch and even more nuanced than many of his other works.

Arc Valley with Viaduct and a Pine Tree, c.1883–5, watercolour and pencil on paper, Graphische Sammlung Albertina, Vienna, Austria, 31 x 49cm (12 x 19in)

Watercolour enabled Cézanne to work out his compositions freely, encouraging him to be a little more unstructured and spontaneous. With delicate, unblended strokes, he achieved a luminosity and harmony that he did not think was possible with oils.

The Aqueduct (Mont Sainte-Victoire Seen through Trees), 1885–7, oil on canvas, Pushkin State Museum of Fine Arts, Moscow, Russia, 91 x 72cm (35 x 28in)

With strong short brushstrokes and bold, bright colours, the blue, green and tawny patches depict the light and forms of the landscape. Cézanne became extremely accomplished at this type of composition – where views beyond are seen through trees. Whereas many other artists refrained from this sort of arrangement, in case the trees became a barrier, Cézanne made them into a speciality.

Women in a Park, 1885–90, pencil on paper, Philade phia Museum of Art, PA, USA, 13 x 22cm (5 x 9in)

Delighted at the birth of his first niece, but unhappy at the death of his father, h s marriage, and the publication of Zola's *The Masterpiece* with the subsequent severance of friendship, the 1880s were particularly challenging for Cézanne. Drawing, with its mechanical demands, helped to take his mind off difficult things. This is one of many of his drawings that record details of domestic life.

View of Gardanne, c.1885–6,
oil on canvas,
Barnes Foundation,
Philadelphia, PA, USA,
64 x 99cm (25 x 39in)

From a distance, Cézanne depicted the town of Gardanne and surrounding countryside, creating a geometric arrangement where even the trees conform to the shapes of the buildings. He said, "Nature is always the same but nothing in her that appears to us lasts. Our art must render the thrill of her permanence, along with her elements, the appearance of all her changes. It must give us a taste of her Eternity."

Self-portrait with a Bowler Hat, c.1883–7, oil on canvas, New Carlsberg Glyptotek, Copenhagen, Denmark, 45 x 36cm (18 x 14in)

Around the middle of the 1860s, Cézanne introduced a characteristic pose into his self-portraits as seen here: looking back over his shoulder at the viewer. In his hat and coat, it appears that he painted it in a hurry, just as he was going out or coming in, but it would have taken him time to build up the patterned brush marks in diagonal dashes.

*Provençal Landscape, c.*1886, oil on canvas, National Museum of Wales, Cardiff, UK, 81 x 66cm (32 x 26in)

With his considerable inheritance, when his father died in 1886, Cézanne's financial problems ended. He still spent much of his time at the Jas de Bouffan, looking after his mother and painting on the estate. This study of a thicket was probably painted there. By the mid- to late 1880s, his brushstrokes had become fairly regular; not the fragmented, blended marks of his Impressionist period, but hatched parallel marks in subtle colour contrasts.

*Flowers and Fruit, c.*1886, oil on canvas, Musée de l'Orangerie, Paris, France, 35 x 21cm (13 x 8in)

Even though Cézanne was unappreciated by the public and critics for most of his life, many artists valued him highly. "How does he do it?" Renoir marvelled. "He can't put two touches of paint on a canvas without success." He also declared, "I don't think you can find any artist who compares with Cézanne in the whole history of painting," while Pissarro said, "If you want to learn to paint, look at Cézanne."

The Road Leading to the Lake, c.1885, oil on canvas, Rijksmuseum Kröller-Müller, Otterlo, The Netherlands, 92 x 75cm (36 x 29in)

In Cézanne's quest to express the three related dimensions to his practice — his way of seeing, his way of organizing what he saw, and its expressiveness — he investigated aspects of science that related to vision and colour. These investigations helped him to move away from conventional ways of seeing and painting. This may be why many elements of his paintings look distorted.

Portrait of Madame Cézanne, 1885, oil on canvas, Philadelphia Museum of Art, PA, USA, 46 x 38cm (18 x 15in)

In her usual hairstyle and dark clothing, Hortense is depicted here at about 35 years old. Uncharacteristically, Cezanne has painted her looking thoughtful, perhaps even wistful. In most of his portraits of her, her mood is unfathomable, but in this painting, her tilted head and lifted chin give her a more assured look. Autumnal coloured leaves against the pale blue sky suggest an outdoor setting.

House in Provence, 1886, oil on canvas, Indianapolis Museum of Art, Indiana, IN, USA, 65 x 81cm (26 x 32in)

Taken from the landscape below Mont Sainte-Victoire, this farmhouse, half protected by trees and crumbling walls, seems isolated and desolate. The shuttered windows and low doors create sharp geometric shapes against the fragmented marks of the landscape. Still seeking to understand the basic structures underlying nature, Cézanne has converted the background into a series of horizontal bands, broken only by a few vertical lines from the house and trees.

Still Life with a Commode, c.1883–7, oil on canvas, Fogg Art Museum, Cambridge, MA, USA, 62 x 79cm (24 x 31in)

With its deep background colouring, the brightness of the foreground objects attracts viewers' attention. The colours and the placement of objects create harmony and contrast: mottled reds and yellows against greens and white; straight lines of the furniture surrounding the curves of the fruit, cloth and pots. This is a stable composition that is much more complex than many of Cézanne's earlier still lifes, but it remains powerful and balanced.

Landscape, 1885, traces of watercolour and pencil on paper, Philadelphia Museum of Art, PA, USA, 13 x 22cm (5 x 9in)

Although largely ignored immediately after his death, Cézanne's drawings have since been reassessed. With diagonal, parallel hatched marks, they echo the brushmarks in his oil paintings, but his subtle modulations of tone and object edges also show a more graphic style. His instinctive perception of nature is demonstrated in his lines and use of the white of the paper as an evocation of space and light.

Farm at the Jas de Bouffan,
*c.*1885, oil on canvas,
Barnes Foundation,
Philadelphia, PA, USA,
58 x 72cm (23 x 28in)

Because the Jas de Bouffan was so familiar to him, Cézanne may have felt comfortable exploring aspects of it that he could

not do with untried scenes, such as the contrasts between the architecture and the surrounding trees. The formal severity of this

composition, with the focal point in the middle distance, is built up with bright colours that contrast with the small, sketchy brushstrokes.

Still Life with Pears, 1885,
oil on canvas,
Private Collection,
38 x 46cm (15 x 18in)

By the mid-1880s, Cézanne began concentrating even more on the surroundings of the objects, making these areas as important as the objects themselves. The spaces between the pears, plate and cloth have been painted with rhythmical, diagonal brushwork that echoes and enhances the heavily rounded forms of the fruit.

Flowers in a Vase, c.1885–8,
oil on canvas,
Private Collection,
46 x 56cm (18 x 22in)

Although similar in subject to *The Blue Vase* (see page 71), this is an entirely different style and serves to show the range that Cézanne used to explore and express his personal perceptions. This in comparison to the other blue vase painting is more asymmetrical and with its looser application of paint, appears uncalculated and more spontaneous, yet both works were planned as carefully as each other.

Standing Male Nude, after Luca Signorelli, 1885–90, pencil and watercolour on paper, Philadelphia Museum of Art, PA, USA, 22 x 13cm (9 x 5in)

The depiction of the male nude was central to academic training in the 19th century and while his education in this skill was limited, Cézanne's studies provided him with a foundation. As one of Cézanne's many studies, this was made after a drawing by Luca Signorelli (first documented 1470–1523). Like nearly all of Cézanne's figures, elements of this can be seen in several of his male bather paintings.

Still Life with Pitcher and Fruit, 1885–7, oil on canvas, Private Collection, 43 x 63cm (17 x 24in)

Cézanne said: "See in nature the cylinder, the sphere, the cone, putting everything into proper perspective, so that each side of an object or a plane is directed toward a central point. Lines parallel to the horizon give breadth, that is, a section of nature... Lines perpendicular to the horizon give depth. But nature, for us men, is more depth than surface."

La Mont Sainte-Victoire,
*c.*1887–90, oil on canvas,
Musée d'Orsay,
Paris, France,
65 x 92cm (25 x 36in)

With his balanced
compositions, by the late
1880s, Cézanne's paintings
no longer followed the laws
of the visible at all. As he
told Bernard: "We must see
nature as if no one had seen
it before us." Increasingly, he
compressed space into an
integrated structure of
intersecting planes as he has
done here with his patterned
brush marks of alternating
warm and cool colours.

Hillside in Provence,
*c.*1886–92, oil on canvas,
National Gallery,
London, UK,
64 x 79 cm (25 x 31in)

The actual location of this
rocky hillside has not been
identified, but it is probable
that the wall of angular,
jutting rock formations may
represent a quarry in
Provence. By this point in his
career, Cézanne was perhaps
more introspective, but also
more confident with his
explorations and contrasts in
paint: complex and simple,
dark and light, curvilinear
and straight, soft and hard,
bright and subtle.

Madame Cézanne, c.1886,
oil on canvas, Detroit
Institute of Arts, MI, USA,
101 x 81cm (40 x 32in)

Once more appearing
frozen, her face mask-like
and built up with colour
'touches,' Hortense sits in
the stable composition of an
icon, her tightly clasped
hands and impassive
expression revealing nothing
of her personality or her
relationship with the artist.
As much as some of his
works can be seen to have
influenced Cubism, this
can be seen as a direct
inspiration to Amedeo
Modigliani (1884–1920).

*Plain in Provence, c.*1886, oil
on canvas, Villa Flora,
Winterthur, Switzerland,
59 x 81cm (23 x 31in)

Patches of saturated colour
laid down with relatively
broad brushstrokes are
juxtaposed and overlapped.
Angled in several directions,
these brushstrokes create
lively rhythms contrary to
the impression of solidity and
permanence that the overall
image imparts. It is apparent
here how Cézanne's
emphasis on analysing
relationships of forms in
space influenced the
development of Cubism
after his death.

Portrait of Madame Cézanne,
c.1886–7, oil on canvas,
Philadelphia Museum of
Art, PA, USA,
46 x 38cm (18 x 15in)

Once owned by Matisse,
the subject of this work is
perhaps more impenetrable
than ever. Hortense's
emotionless face, dark

clothing and severe hairstyle
offer viewers no indication
of her personality or
emotional state. Yet the
painting is a spectacle

of multiple hues in
various tones, applied in
constructive strokes and
in thin, delicate marks of
unblended pigment.

The Avenue in Chantilly, 1888, oil on canvas, Toledo Museum of Art, OH, USA, 81 x 65cm (32 x 26in)

According to Paul Cézanne junior, his father spent five months in Chantilly. While there, he painted about five works and he gave this to Vollard in 1899. This work has been gently but firmly painted with a broad range of contrasting colours, including blues, greens, golds, orange, yellow and violet. The central, symmetrical composition is unique to him and emphasizes the blue slate roofs at vanishing point.

View of the Domaine St Joseph, c.1887, oil on canvas, Metropolitan Museum of Art, New York, NY, USA, 65 x 81cm (26 x 32in)

As one of the few paintings that Cézanne signed, even though there are areas of blank canvas, it can be assumed that he considered the work finished. The location is the Colline des Pauvres, on the road between Aix and the village of Le Tholonet, and his method is reminiscent of his earlier Impressionist style. This could be a direct result of his painting with Renoir around Aix that year.

Four Bathers, 1888, oil on canvas, Ny Carlsberg Glyptotek, Copenhagen, Denmark, 72 x 92cm (28 x 36in)

The subtly modulated constructive strokes of earlier bather paintings have been replaced with bold dashes. The foliage and figures seem to be pushed forward, but the small triangle of blue sky creates a feeling of energy. The bathers are solid, rounded and dramatic – and they were 'borrowed' in later works by younger artists, such as Matisse and Picasso.

The Banks of the Marne,
1888, oil on canvas, State
Hermitage Museum,
St Petersburg, Russia,
65 x 81cm (26 x 32in)

Unlike the Impressionists and
other painters of the open
air, Cézanne's images of
water are still, almost solid.
Reflections do not shimmer
and change is not recorded,
as he sought to capture
permanence. Once more
this is a stable composition,
framed by trees. The
brushstrokes follow every
form, appearing deceptively
sketchy, but in actuality,
they were extremely
carefully applied.

Pot of Flowers and Pears,
1888–90, oil on canvas,
Courtauld Institute
Galleries, London, UK,
46 x 56cm (18 x 22in)

The edge of the table top is
at different heights as it
passes behind the objects.
This is because Cézanne
wanted to unify the table
with the slant of the canvas.
Distortions like this were
deliberate. He was not
looking for underlying
geometric forms on which
to construct his images, but
wanted to remind viewers
that everything stems from
these basic structures.

The Kitchen Table, 1888–90, oil on canvas, Musée d'Orsay, Paris, France, 65 x 80cm (26 x 31in)

Although looking as if they have been tossed on the table randomly, Cézanne placed every object carefully. With his perceptive gaze, he created both impact and equilibrium in the painting, choosing viewpoints for each object so he could produce his understanding of depth, solidity and weight. After close, intense study, he built up small areas, across the canvas, developing this modulated effect on every object, which has each been painted in a particular size to create balance within the work.

The Banks of the Marne, c.1888, oil on canvas, Pushkin State Museum of Fine Art, Moscow, Russia, 71 x 90cm (28 x 35in)

Cézanne would not speak of modelling, but of modulation – which described his changes of colour on each object to create apparent solidity and weight. Here, repetitive brushstrokes in subtle nuances of colour are used to explore both the land masses and the reflections. He took such care with every canvas because, as he once told Denis, "I wanted to make of Impressionism something solid and enduring like the art in museums."

Portrait of Madame Cézanne,
1888, oil on canvas,
Museum of Fine Arts,
Houston, TX, USA,
74 x 61cm (29 x 24in)

The term objective analysis
springs to mind on viewing
this image. Once again
Cézanne has studied his wife
with detached observation,
simplifying the forms of her
limbs, body and head. The
image is calm, painted
predominantly in blues and
browns; her head is still
but the background and
her collar are portrayed with
more animation, cascading
and curving in ripples
and scrolls.

*Madame Cézanne in a Yellow
Armchair,* 1888–90, oil on
canvas, Fondation Beyeler,
Riehen-Basel, Switzerland,
81 x 65cm (31 x 25in)

Cézanne painted three
versions of this portrait: his
wife in a yellow damask-
covered armchair, wearing a
red dress. Her features are
simplified and her hands
are not fully articulated; the
entire image has been built
up with vibrant dabs of
colour. Essentially made up
of the three primary colours
– the red dress, the yellow
chair and the blue wall –
there are actually myriad
hues in the composition.

Mont Sainte-Victoire, 1888, oil on canvas, Courtauld Institute Galleries, London, UK, 67 x 92cm (26 x 36in)

A practically identical view to the one on page 78, this is seen from a point to the west of Aix, about 13 km (8 miles) from the mountain peak. With some suggestion of texture in more agitated brush marks than usual and soft nuances of colour, Cézanne also primed the canvas in light cream and has allowed this to show through in parts, which adds to the overall luminosity of the painting.

Woman with a Green Hat, 1888, oil on canvas, Barnes Foundation, Philadelphia, PA, USA, 98 x 80cm (39 x 31in)

As usual with Cézanne's works, he has created contrasts but displayed them harmoniously. The integration of colour and light works like a rhythmic pattern across the canvas, while the shapes, such as the curves of the chair arms, are echoed in her hat, and horizontal lines are picked out in the dado rail behind the chair, the top of the chair itself and a line across the woman's jacket.

Pierrot and Harlequin, 1888, oil on canvas, Pushkin State Museum of Fine Arts, Moscow, Russia, 102 x 81cm (40 x 32in)

Also called *Mardi Gras*, the subject was taken from the popular Italian theatre of Commedia dell'Arte. Sixteen-year-old Paul posed for his father as Harlequin, and his friend Louis Guillaume was Pierrot. The figures of Pierrot and Harlequin have been portrayed by many artists, but usually in a carefree and lively manner. Cézanne has instead given the boys a stiff and unnatural appearance.

House at Bellevue, 1888–92, oil on canvas, Museum Folkwang, Essen, Germany, 65 x 81cm (26 x 32in)

In 1881, Cézanne's sister Rose had married Maxime Conil who owned Montbriant, a farm to the west of Aix. In December 1886, after the death of Louis-Auguste Cézanne, Rose used her share of the inheritance to buy a neighbouring farm, Bellevue, for 38,000 francs. Cézanne painted his sister and brother-in-law's house at least eight times, in oils and in watercolours.

Pigeon House at Bellevue,
*c.*1888–92, oil on canvas,
Private Collection,
Switzerland,
60 x 81cm (23 x 31in)

Bellevue, standing on a hillside, with its fine view of the Arc valley across to Mont Sainte-Victoire, was one of Cézanne's favourite places to paint. From a low viewpoint, he used his methods of intense study through a searching gaze and a determined effort to portray his visual and inner perceptions to produce a landscape and view of a building of quiet dignity.

Country House by a River,
1888–90, oil on canvas,
Israel Museum,
Jerusalem, Israel,
81 x 65cm (32 x 25in)

In this mature landscape, using a traditional symmetrical composition, Cézanne simplified forms and shapes, building them up with a profuse number of colours that he mixed from his limited palette. Once again, even his watery reflections appear solid and stable because of the ways in which he has used colour. Using a mature form of his constructional brushstrokes, the composition is calm and controlled.

Still Life of Peaches and Pears, 1888–9, oil on canvas, Pushkin State Museum of Fine Arts, Moscow, Russia, 60 x 90cm (24 x 35in)

With his shifting perspectives and changing viewpoints, this still life shows viewers more of each object than a straightforward single-point perspective image. Cézanne observed: "Lines parallel to the horizon give breadth… But nature for us men is more depth than surface, whence the need to introduce into our light vibrations, represented by the reds and yellows, a sufficient amount of blueness to give the feel of air."

Still Life with Bottle of Liqueur, c.1888–90, oil on canvas, Private Collection, 57 x 66cm (22 x 26in)

Cézanne treated every subject in the same way. His intention was to make viewers aware through his technique that they were looking at an image on a two-dimensional canvas – no dishonest pretence of illusion. To this end, he spent days studying all his still life arrangements. This rich grouping of colours and shapes was treated in the same way; intense observation and careful rendering of forms from various viewpoints.

Harlequin, 1888–90, oil on canvas, National Gallery of Art, Washington, DC, USA, 92 x 65cm (39 x 25in)

As in the *Pierrot and Harlequin (see page 196),* Paul posed for Harlequin. In this work, his face has been painted as an impassive mask as Cézanne focused on the costume, hat, wooden sword and isolation of the solitary figure. It resembles some of his portraits of Hortense as he concentrated on the figure and background to create the most harmonious image.

Pigeon Tower at Bellevue,
1888–92, oil on canvas,
Kunsthalle, Basel,
Switzerland,
64 x 80cm (25 x 31in)

"I am passionately fond of the contours of this country," Cézanne wrote. Although his style changed, his aims remained essentially the same. Between 1888 and 1892, he painted three views of the pigeon tower at the Conils' house in Bellevue. To make the tower the focal point of the composition, he exaggerated its solid, cylindrical shape by extending it and placing it against the darker tones of the trees.

Pigeon Tower at Bellevue, 1889–90, oil on canvas, Cleveland Museum of Art, OH, USA, 66 x 82cm (26 x 32in)

Providing a safe haven for Cézanne during the 1880s, Bellevue was a place he returned to frequently. He explored the surrounding terrain, but it was only toward the end of the decade that he turned his attention to the buildings on the estate. Sheltered by cypress, olive and pine trees, this pigeon tower at the property's highest point was one of the most distinctive features.

Self-portrait with a Soft Hat, 1890–4, oil on canvas, Bridgestone Museum of Art, Tokyo, Japan, 60 x 50cm (24 x 20in)

Leaving patches of canvas primed in cream showing through his brush marks, Cézanne painted himself from his usual angle, turned to the side and looking over his right shoulder. To most of his contemporaries, his work seemed beyond comprehension, but to modern eyes, this picture can be seen as a precursor to Expressionism, Cubism and several other 20th-century movements.

The Boy in the Red Vest,
1889–90, pencil and
watercolour on paper,
Private Collection,
46 x 30cm (18 x 12in)

From 1888 to 1890,
Cézanne and his family lived
in Paris on the Île Saint-Louis.
The significant fortune left
to him by his father meant
that he could afford a
decent apartment and to
pay for occasional models.
This model was named
Michelangelo di Rosa and he
appears in four of Cézanne's
paintings. It might look loose,
but this portrait was not a
sketch, rather a complete
painting on its own.

The Boy in the Red Waistcoat,
1888–90, oil on canvas,
E. G. Bührle Collection,
Zürich, Switzerland,
80 x 65cm (31 x 26in)

This young Italian peasant,
who worked as Cézanne's
model, sits thoughtfully
against a green, white and
blue background, wearing a
red waistcoat, blue scarf and
white shirt. The bold colours
contrast directly with the
pensive mood portrayed.
Although he was still
exploring construction,
Cézanne has unusually
also focused on a more
subjective execution,
featuring the sitter's mood in
a tightly controlled pattern of
intersecting diagonals.

Fruit and Jug on a Table,
*c.*1890–4, oil on canvas,
Museum of Fine Arts,
Boston, MA, USA,
32 x 41cm (13 x 16in)

The careful positioning of
each object creates a
powerful sense of tension.
Cézanne's later still lifes all
appear distorted because he
portrayed them from subtly
shifting viewpoints. Unlike
the lifelike Dutch still lifes he
admired, he emphasized the
difference between three-
dimensional reality and
two-dimensional paintings.
He called these works
"constructions from nature,"
stressing the underlying
geometry of all the shapes
and negative spaces.

Fruit on a Cloth, 1890,
oil on canvas, Bridgestone
Museum of Art,
Tokyo, Japan,
38 x 46cm (15 x 18in)

Toward the end of his life,
Cézanne confessed to having
difficulty in seeing edges
clearly. It is possible that
he suffered from a kind of
astigmatism, which is why
he often made his verticals
slope. In this work, he
emphasized contours,
making them crisp and
precise, with colours starkly
illuminated against the white
cloth. He was always careful
to place contrasting and
complementary colours
against each other.

Kettle and Fruit, 1888–90, oil on canvas, present whereabouts unknown, 50 x 61cm (19 x 24in)

"Art which isn't based on feeling isn't art at all… feeling is the principle, the beginning and the end; craft, objective, technique – all these are in the middle", Cézanne declared. In 1914, Kandinsky observed of his still lifes: "He gives to them a colourful expression, which establishes an artistic, inner note and moulds them into the form, elevating them to abstract sounding notes of harmony, radiating mathematical formulae."

Still Life with Apples and Primroses, 1890–4, oil on canvas, Metropolitan Museum of Art, New York, NY, USA, 73 x 92cm (28 x 36in)

Becoming increasingly remote, Cézanne concentrated even more on his still lifes. His friend Numa Coste wrote to Zola in the early 1890s: "[Cézanne] is well and physically solid, but he has become timid and younger than ever. He lives at the Jas de Bouffan with his mother who…is on bad terms with the Ball [Cézanne's friends' nickname for Hortense], who in turn, does not get on with her sisters-in-law."

*Portrait of Madame Cézanne in a Red Dress, c.*1890–4, oil on canvas, Museu de Arte, São Paulo, Brazil, 89 x 70cm (35 x 27in)

Although the dates attributed to the three paintings of Hortense in the yellow armchair vary, it is likely that they – and this – were produced at around the same time, as Hortense is wearing the same red dress. By the 1890s, Cézanne was proficient in describing forms in space through his many touches of paint, and these portraits were for him an exercise in exploring that skill further.

Woman with a Coffee Pot, c.1890–5, oil on canvas, Musée d'Orsay, Paris, France, 131 x 97cm (52 x 38in)

It is believed that the model for this portrait was one of the employees at the Jas de Bouffan. Echoing the woman's upright stance are the cup, spoon and coffee pot, with horizontal lines in the panelling balancing this. As with everything Cézanne painted at this time, viewpoints change across the canvas, for instance, the table top is seen from above, while the woman and coffee pot are seen from the side.

Still Life with Aubergines, 1893–4, oil on canvas, Metropolitan Museum of Art, New York, NY, USA, 73 x 92cm (28 x 36in)

Cézanne's still lifes became more distorted-looking as he matured. Increasingly complex arrangements of familiar objects such as these meant that he could focus on changing viewpoints. The raffia-corded ginger jar, for example (featured in over 11 other works), is seen from the side and also from a higher viewpoint at the top, while the plate is angled from the side and the lemon is seen head-on.

Madame Cézanne in a Yellow Armchair, 1888–94, oil on canvas, Art Institute of Chicago, IL, USA, 81 x 65cm (32 x 26in)

In comparison to one of the other versions of this portrait (see page 194), this painting is a little more worked up. Hortense's features, although simplified, are more stylized and although her expression again is remote and inscrutable, it is nonetheless more human than in previous portraits. The angled image of his wife in her red dress sitting in the yellow armchair exudes the serenity of a religious icon.

Under the Branches near the Jas de Bouffan, 1890–4, oil on canvas, Private Collection, 65 x 92cm (25 x 36in)

Cézanne often created landscapes at close proximity with no sky. This composition is formed by diagonal and vertical lines, softened by a mass of foliage that fills about half of the canvas like a canopy, heightening the effects of pattern and contrast. Contrast is further emphasized with different types of paint application – firm, forceful strokes for the tree trunks and softer, crosshatched patches in the leaves.

The Card Players, 1890, pencil and watercolour on paper, Rhode Island Museum of Art, Providence, RI, USA, 49 x 36cm (19 x 14in)

Between about 1890 and 1896, Cézanne produced his card player pictures. He probably chose the subject because the people playing cards (usually workers from the Jas de Bouffan) remained essentially still. This drawing, with a few discreet touches of blue watercolour to indicate the colour of the smock, is one of his sketches for a final painting. Light shines across the man's face as he sits in motionless contemplation.

Study for the Card Players,
c.1890–2, oil on canvas,
Worcester Art
Museum, MA, USA,
32 x 35cm (12 x 14 in)

With small brushstrokes,
Cézanne built up a complex
organization of planes of
colour to describe the man
intent on his hand of cards.
It is a vigorous painting of a
simple subject; in firm, short
marks Cézanne conveyed
the bulk of the man's body,
the feeling of peace that
pervades the room as he
concentrates on his next
move and the soft lighting
that surrounds him.

Tile-roof House in Landscape,
1890–4, oil on canvas,
Barnes Foundation,
Philadelphia, PA, USA,
55 x 79cm (22 x 31in)

The evolution of Cézanne's
style is not linear or
continuous. As with many
of the works in this book, he
often tried out something –
such as constructional
brushstrokes – and then
reverted back to an earlier
approach or blended a
couple of methods at once.
Gradually, his distinctive style
emerged and this unfinished
painting reveals something of
that technique. His marks
are careful, directional,
multi-toned and layered.

House with a Red Roof,
1887–90, oil on canvas,
Private Collection,
73 x 92cm (28 x 36in)

The bright palette and
free handling that Cézanne
had developed in Paris
with Pissarro and the
Impressionists emerged
once again in this work,
although he blended it with
his later methods of more
constructional touches and
even more nuances of
colour. This is the Jas de
Bouffan. It features his
characteristically leaning
vertical and horizontal lines
and deliberately incorrect
proportions.

*Still Life with Bottles and
Peaches,* 1890, oil on
canvas, Stedelijk Museum,
Amsterdam,
The Netherlands,
49 x 51cm (19 x 20in)

Once again reverting to his
more Impressionistic style,
this softly rendered still life
nevertheless retains the
strength and conviction
of Cézanne's later work.
The painting is probably
unfinished, with several areas
of the primed canvas
showing through the thin
applications of paint;
Cézanne may have intended
to return to it at some point
or perhaps he felt less than
satisfied with the almost
square composition.

Still Life with Milk Jug and Fruit on a Table, 1890, oil on canvas, Nasjonalgalleriet, Oslo, Norway, 60 x 73cm (24 x 29in)

Cézanne's multiple viewpoints can be seen clearly in this still life, with his harmonious colours once again placed in patches to convey every element of the work. He rarely applied outlines, only using occasional broken lines in different lengths and thicknesses to imply shadow rather than contour. The effects he was aiming for are reinforced by the emphatic quality of his brushstrokes.

*Peasant, c.*1891, oil on canvas, Private Collection, 56 x 46cm (22 x 18in)

Cézanne needed a week of daily sessions just to sketch the outline of his models and to indicate a few shadows and colours, so he demanded great patience from them. This portrait is striking for its boldness, with black outlines and shadows and a predominantly blue palette. It shows clearly how he influenced younger artists such as Van Gogh.

Great Pine near Aix, 1890–5, oil on canvas, State Hermitage Museum, St Petersburg, Russia, 72 x 91cm (28 x 35in)

Pine trees often appear in Cézanne's paintings, but the solitary pine was a less frequent theme. The way in which he painted this — executed on the Montbriant property belonging to the Conils that overlooked the valley and small village of Bellevue — shows his reverence for the trees. His viewpoint is close and results in a cross-shaped composition that emphasizes the patterns made by the branches.

Four Peaches on a Plate, oil on canvas, 1890–4, Barnes Foundation, Philadelphia, PA, USA, 24 x 36cm (9 x 14in)

With obvious slanting brushwork to build the impression of three-dimensional volume in the fruit and fabric behind, Cézanne used an extremely subtle blend of many different tones and colours. With the fruit in close up, this painting appears to vibrate with colour and texture. The clarity of individual marks creates an impression of both richness and delicacy, illustrating the fruit in terms of solidity, texture, colour, contour and tone.

Boat and Bathers, c.1890, oil on canvas, Musée de l'Orangerie, Paris, France, 30 x 125cm (11 x 49in)

Featuring both soft and bright colours, this long, slim canvas shows a combination of Cézanne's Impressionist style and his later, more solid, small brush marks placed in conjunction with each other. The sky and silhouetted boats help to impart the notion of width while the trees and bathers on each side help to bind the whole scene together. This was possibly painted for Chocquet's new house in Paris.

Great Trees at the Jas de Bouffan, 1890, oil on canvas, Private Collection, 73 x 59cm (28 x 23in)

A clear example of Cézanne's parallel touch, this is one of his completed canvases, although as usual, he has not signed it. Small, carefully placed brush marks have been aligned across the foliage in two directions, creating powerful diagonals against the densely painted tree trunks and ground. With parallel, oblong strokes, he evoked a powerful sense of tension while also conveying stability and harmony.

Seated Boy, 1890–5, oil on canvas, Private Collection, 39 x 49cm (15 x 19in)

Only occasionally in Cézanne's landscapes do his figures appear to have actually posed for him out of doors. Here it seems that he tried to coax his son to sit for him and probably only achieved it on one occasion as this sketch documents. The canvas demonstrates how he worked. With the tip of a brush and fairly dry paint, he sketched in some basic contours before layering on colour.

The Smoker, 1891–2, oil on canvas, Städtische Kunsthalle, Mannheim, Germany, 93 x 74cm (37 x 29in)

Cézanne painted three versions of Alexandre Paulin, leaning on his hand, smoking a small white clay pipe. He is sitting in the kitchen of the Jas de Bouffan, leaning on a table covered in the brown tablecloth seen in *The Card Players.* His diagonal pose is reinforced by the marks on his clothes, the angle of his fingers and the contrasts of line in the surroundings.

The Smoker, 1890–5, oil on canvas, State Hermitage Museum, St Petersburg, Russia, 93 x 74cm (37 x 29in)

In this version of Paulin smoking, a small still life is behind his elbow; his hat is pushed back on his head and his suit has been interpreted in grey tones.

Perhaps because of the sunnier colours and emphasis on diagonals, this painting appears less sombre than the version shown above. Cézanne possibly referred to this subject when he said, "Most of all, I love the appearance of those who have aged without ever changing their habits."

Girl with a Doll, c.1902,
oil on canvas,
Private Collection,
96 x 72cm (38 x 28in)

By the turn of the 20th century, Cézanne's struggle toward recognition was beginning to pay off. Yet despite the fact that he was attracting a firm following of admirers, he was still being attacked in the press. It was not just the vitriolic comments by journalists that hurt and disturbed him, but also the threatening letters and anonymous insults that he received.

The Card Players, 1893–6, oil on canvas, Musée d'Orsay, Paris, France, 47 x 56cm (18 x 22in)

Cézanne had seen the painting *The Card Players,* attributed to the Le Nain brothers, at the museum in Aix. This probably gave him the idea for this subject. Here, the bottle forms the central axis of the composition, separating the space into two halves, accentuating the direct opposition of the players. In his effort to achieve a balanced interaction, he harmonized the colour range and used vertical, horizontal and diagonal lines to create tension in the pictorial structure.

Peasant in a Blue Smock, 1892 or 1897, oil on canvas, Kimbell Art Museum, Fort Worth, TX, USA, 81 x 65cm (31 x 25in)

This labourer from the Jas de Bouffan also posed for *The Card Players.* Blues and oranges contrast with each other and dominate the image, and the man is depicted as motionless with his gaze fixed beyond the canvas. Cézanne's young friend Gasquet wrote of this: "In the Jas de Bouffan studio there are some canvases of robust peasants resting from their work, their complexions nourished by the sun, their shoulders powerful."

Drinker, 1891, oil on canvas,
Barnes Foundation,
Philadelphia, PA, USA,
46 x 37cm (18 x 15in)

In another depiction of
another Jas de Bouffan
labourer, Cézanne has
applied vivid blue under the
brown of the man's clothes.
Where this shows through,
the colours seem more
vibrant – a trick employed
by the Venetian Mannerists
of the 16th century. With
broken black strokes used as
contour and shadow lines,
plus varied viewpoints, this is
reminiscent of the style of
several of his later paintings
of Mont Sainte-Victoire.

Potted Plants, 1891–2, oil on
canvas, Barnes Foundation,
Philadelphia, PA, USA,
14 x 11cm (35 x 28in)

The proximity of the objects
to the picture plane is an
unusual departure for
Cézanne. Creating strong
patterns and contrasts
with vertical, horizontal
and oblique shapes and
curvilinear organic forms, he
has differentiated between
objects by using dark
contours and a variety of
predominantly green hues.
The red scarf between the
left-hand pot and bottle
helps to project the objects
toward the viewer.

*Small Green Jug, c.*1885–7,
pencil and watercolour
on paper, Musée du
Louvre, Paris, France,
22 x 24cm (8 x 9in)

Most of Cézanne's
watercolours are studies,
examining the problems of
image-making he explored
more frequently in oils.
At this time, he felt his
meticulous brushstrokes
made his work appear too
busy, so he used watercolour
to attain the effects he
sought far more simply. For
this period, he also often
limited his watercolour
palette to green, blue and
some warm earth colours.

*Mont Sainte-Victoire Seen
from Gardanne,* 1892–5,
oil on canvas, Yokohama
Museum of Art, Japan,
73 x 92cm (28 x 36in)

Painted almost in the
ethereal colours of the
Impressionists, this painting
nonetheless shows none of
the ephemeral effects they
achieved. The structure of
the land is clearly delineated,
as Cézanne painted with
short, agitated brush marks,
emphasizing the undulating
surface and the underlying
contours of the area. It was
an unusual departure for him
to use such soft colours, but
as the work is unfinished it
could be that he intended
to build up stronger colours
with subsequent layers
of paint.

Compotier, Pitcher and Fruit,
c.1892–4, oil on canvas,
Barnes Foundation,
Philadelphia, PA, USA,
73 x 92cm (29 x 36in)

Combining two of Cézanne's
favourite compositions, the
pyramid and a step-like
arrangement, this large still
life features many of his
familiar, mature style devices.
The table top recedes and
forms a steep angle with the
background, while the angle
of the table creates a
dynamic impression, with
the white folded tablecloth
rising in a peak like a
mountain in a landscape.

*Millstone in the Park of the
Château Noir,* 1892–4, oil on
canvas, Philadelphia Museum
of Art, PA, USA,
73 x 92cm (28 x 36in)

By this point in Cézanne's
career, his constructional
brushstrokes, application of
tone and blend of pigment
to create a variety of shades
had reached a point of
precision. The woods
surrounding the Château
Noir were in some parts
almost impenetrable, so
few walkers passed, allowing
Cézanne as much time in
solitude as he needed to
explore his ideals through
the scattered rocks and
lush greenery.

Still Life with Plaster Cast,
*c.*1894, oil on canvas,
Courtauld Institute
Galleries, London, UK,
71 x 57cm (28 x 22in)

There are ambiguities
everywhere in this still life.
For instance, the plaster
Cupid (portrayed from a
cast of Puget's Cupid)
appears far larger than it
actually is; the apple across
the floor is as large as those
in the foreground; the
painting leaning on the wall is
also portrayed larger than it
is and the floor slopes quite
dramatically. The cloth at
the bottom merges with the
painting behind and
the table top by the onion
blends into the floor.

Still Life with Blue Drapery,
*c.*1893–4, oil on canvas,
Private Collection,
42 x 72cm (17 x 28in)

In the early to mid-1890s,
Cézanne was confident that
his approach was achieving
something, but as he did
throughout his life, he again
referred to the earlier artists
he admired. In this series of
paintings, he once more
began referring to Chardin
with pairings of objects that
complement each other
through contrasts, such as
the folds of the blue fabric
against the smooth
rectilinear table.

Rocks in the Forest, c.1893–4, oil on canvas, Metropolitan Museum of Art, New York, NY, USA, 73 x 92cm (29 x 36in)

During the mid-1890s, Cézanne began working with fairly thin paint, closer to his watercolour application than his earlier oils. The location is believed to be the Forest of Fontainebleau, which had been used by several earlier landscape painters. Cézanne was the first to paint the large grey-violet rocks that are strewn throughout the forest against the Scotch pine trees with their straight trunks and reddish bark.

Fruit and Blue Drapery, c.1890–3, oil on canvas, Barnes Foundation, Philadelphia, PA, USA, 25 x 36cm (10 x 14in)

In this unfinished work, Cézanne has concentrated on the objects' solidity, weight and opacity. The darkness of the heavy, blue patterned fabric has the effect of throwing the boldly coloured fruit forward, but most of all, although fabric has been draped in paintings for centuries, this seems to have no precedent; it is an original and rhythmical arrangement that emphasizes simplicity.

Mont Sainte-Victoire, c.1894,
oil on canvas,
Cleveland Museum
of Art, OH, USA,
72 x 92cm (28 x 36in)

During the last 20 years of
his life, Cézanne repeatedly
painted the towering
mountain of Sainte-Victoire.
He became obsessed with it
and painted it over 60 times
with increasing freedom.
Here, he has shaped the
tree branch in the
foreground to echo the
shape of the distant
mountain. A sense of space
and depth has been created
through rhythmic strokes
and slabs of warm and
cool colours.

Winter Landscape, Giverny,
1894, oil on canvas,
Philadelphia Museum of
Art, PA, USA,
65 x 55cm (25 x 31in)

In 1894, Cézanne visited
Monet in Giverny, staying in
a local hotel where he met
other artists including Mary
Cassatt, Renoir and Rodin.
He left this unfinished
painting of an orchard by
the hotel in his room.

*Mont Sainte-Victoire View
from the Grove of Château
Noir, c.1904, oil on canvas,
Edsel and Eleanor Ford
House, Grosse Pointe
Shores, MI, USA,
65 x 80cm (25 x 31in)*

Cézanne applied
transformations of colour in
contrasting directions across
the canvas. Working on
an off-white ground,
without any preliminary
pencil sketch, he covered
the canvas with a vibrant
net of rich variations
of blues, greys, mauves
and greens, creating an
unusual texture that
animates the surface.
Seen from the grove
to the east of Château
Noir, Mont Sainte-
Victoire rises above a
succession of hills.

*Chimney at the Entrance to
the Forest, c.1879, oil on
canvas, Private Collection,
56 x 46cm (22 x 18in)*

From the 1870s to his last
years, Cézanne obsessively
explored trees, woodlands,
forests, thickets and foliage.
This work, with its effect of
being painted rapidly *en plein
air*, was produced about
20 years before the other
paintings on this page.
Demonstrating his
Impressionist style, it
features a harmonious
palette applied in short,
parallel, diagonal
brushstrokes, which
anticipate his later
landscapes. Only the
apparent spontaneity of
execution contrasts with
the rigorously structured
later works.

Bibémus: Red Rock, c.1895–7,
oil on canvas, Musée de
l'Orangerie, Paris, France,
92 x 68cm (6 x 26in)

Bibémus is between Aix and
Mont Sainte-Victoire. It is
one of the many ancient
quarries in the mountains of
Provence. Cézanne spent
time exploring Bibémus in
his youth with Zola and
Baille, but it was not until
he was much older that he
began to paint there.
The distinctive orange
stone was particularly
striking against the dense,
dark green vegetation
and the forms were
both monumental
and atmospheric.

Still Life, c.1895, oil on
canvas, Private Collection,
46 x 61cm (18 x 24in)

With heavily marked
contours and thinly applied
paint, this still life marks
another development in
Cézanne's methods. It was
probably painted after he
had visited an exhibition
of Monet's paintings of
Rouen Cathedral, where
he was impressed by the
atmospherics his friend had
depicted through colour and
line. Similarly, this
work seems to explore
sculptural weight alongside
light, colour and volume.

Peaches and Pears, c.1895,
oil on canvas, Barnes
Foundation, Philadelphia,
PA, USA,
37 x 44cm (15 x 17in)

With a brilliantly coloured palette, probably consisting of white, black, three yellows, three blues, three greens and two reds, Cézanne has once again exploited various colour theories here. Warm and cool pigments and complementary colours are juxtaposed, so vibrant reactions occur. All the Impressionists and the Post-Impressionists investigated these combinations.

Apples and Oranges,
*c.*1895–9, oil on canvas,
Musée d'Orsay,
Paris, France,
74 x 93cm (29 x 36in)

By the mid-1890s, Cézanne's
still lifes had become, not
only complex, but also far
more important to his
development than before.
This forms part of a series of
six that he produced in his
Parisian studio at this time.
Each painting features the
same accessories: china
dishes, a floral-patterned jug
and a draped cloth. Here,
arranged around a diagonal
line across the canvas, the
objects, perceived from
different viewpoints, appear
to tilt forward.

Large Vase in the Garden,
*c.*1895, oil on canvas,
Private Collection,
65 x 54cm (25 x 21in)

Painted with smooth and
juicy paint and swirling brush
marks, this is another
departure in Cézanne's
repertoire and one that
marks him as a pioneer of
abstraction. With its
decorative composition and
carefully arranged colour
scheme, this was probably
painted after he had spent
time with Monet – and it
was possibly inspired by his
garden and some of
his canvases at Giverny.

Ginger Jar and Fruit,
1895–1900, oil on canvas,
Barnes Foundation,
Philadelphia, PA, USA,
72 x 59cm (28 x 23in)

The unifying parallel brush
marks that Cézanne
had been using became
even more closely-knit
in this compact and vivid
arrangement. His use
of colour and tonal
combinations are more
complex and daring than
many of his previous still
lifes. With the benefit of
hindsight, the distorted
angles and perspectives,
linear markings and broken
brushwork can be seen to
be a precursor of Cubism.

Table, Napkin and Fruit,
1895–1900, oil on canvas,
Barnes Foundation,
Philadelphia, PA, USA,
44 x 54cm (17 x 21in)

The ripe, plump fruit
appears to be about to fall
off the canvas, as space and
depth has been created
through planes of colour and
fluid contours and shadows.
Many perspectives dominate
the composition and
although the appearance
seems simple, the
arrangement is as intricate
as many still lifes painted by
earlier artists that Cézanne
admired so much.

Portrait of Gustave Geffroy,
1895, oil on canvas, Musée
d'Orsay, Paris, France,
116 x 89cm (45 x 35in)

During his career, Gustave
Geffroy wrote several
articles praising Cézanne's
work. As a gesture of thanks,
Cézanne painted his
portrait in the spring of
1895. Geffroy's figure forms
a triangular composition
in the centre of the
canvas, surrounded by
the paraphernalia of his
working life. But Cézanne
could not believe in the
sincerity of Geffroy's praise
and never finished the
painting. Nevertheless, it
inspired many younger artists
with its unusual perspectives.

The Glade, 1890–5, oil on
canvas, Toledo Museum
of Art, OH, USA,
100 x 81cm (39 x 32in)

In a letter to Gasquet,
Cézanne wrote, "…art can
never copy nature in the
sense that it can contain the
same colours as those which
exist in the natural scene; it
can only ever produce
colours whose relationships
with one another are like,
not the same as the
relationships between the
colours to be seen in
nature." As can be seen
here, he imitated nature's
colouring as well as he could.

Self-portrait, c.1895,
pencil and watercolour on
paper, Private Collection,
28 x 26cm (11 x 10in)

This is the only known
watercolour self-portrait by
Cézanne and a study for an
oil painting. His constructive
planes and volumes are less
angular than they had been
and the entire portrait is
more fluid than usual. His
patches of colour have no
definite outline and colours
have been allowed to run
into each other in places,
creating modulations and a
softer overall appearance.

Portrait of Joachim Gasquet,
1896, oil on canvas,
Narodni Galerie, Prague,
Czech Republic,
66 x 55cm (26 x 22in)

In this unfinished portrait,
Gasquet appears much
older than his 23 years. His
admiration of Cézanne's
paintings invigorated the
artist and he painted
Gasquet's father Henri at
the same time. Joachim
wrote about the early days
of their friendship: "I saw
him every day. He
brought me to the Jas de
Bouffan, showed me his
canvases. We took long
walks together…"

Lac d'Annecy, 1896, oil on canvas, Courtauld Institute Galleries, London, UK, 65 x 81cm (25 x 32in)

With no sky, and painted with strong directional strokes, predominantly in mellow blues and greens, Cézanne produced this during his second visit to Switzerland when he stayed at the small town of Talloires, on Lake Annecy. He wrote to a friend from there: "I am doing some painting to stop being bored. It isn't very enjoyable but the lake is very fine with big hills all around."

*The Orchard, c.*1895, oil on canvas, pencil and watercolour on paper, Jan Krugier and Marie-Anne Krugier-Poniatowski Collection, Geneva, Switzerland 33 x 47cm (13 x 18in)

One of Cézanne's observations was, "Drawing and colour are not separate at all; in so far as you paint, you draw. The more the colour harmonizes, the more exact the drawing becomes. When colour achieves richness, the form attains its fullness also. The contrasts and connections of tones – there you have the secret of drawing and modelling." In this work, Cézanne fused his pencil lines with his clear colours.

The Road at Marines,
*c.*1896, oil on canvas,
Barnes Foundation,
Philadelphia, PA, USA,
64 x 96cm (25 x 38in)

Parallel horizontal bands and stripes of contrasting colours make up the foreground of this painting, receding into the distance.

Cézanne's brushstrokes are not as apparent as in many other works, and they do not follow the surfaces and elements they depict as

obviously as usual, so the appearance of solidity is not so pronounced. Changes in colour are gradual and only slightly varied in tone.

Bibémus Quarry, 1898–1900,
oil on canvas,
Private Collection,
65 x 54cm (26 x 21in)

Most of Cézanne's pictures
of the Bibémus Quarry are
painted in bold shapes and
colours to emphasize the
massive clefts, dark green
undergrowth and orange-
gold rocks. But this painting,
in contrast with several
others of the same subject,
resembled his softer style of
the early 1870s. The
overgrown and desolate
quality of the quarry
appealed to Cézanne's
preference for solitude.

Man with Skull, 1896–8,
oil on canvas, Barnes
Foundation, Philadelphia,
PA, USA,
127 x 95cm (50 x 37in)

Although most of Cézanne's
works deliberately avoided
any suggestion of emotion,
particularly his portraits,
some of his later works
began to lose that total
objectivity. This painting, for
instance, of a young man
sitting at a table by a skull,
has distinct melancholy
overtones. Muted, sombre
hues intensify this
atmosphere and, along with
the inclusion of the skull, this
may reflect the fact that
Cézanne's health was
deteriorating.

Rocks near the Caves above the Château Noir, c.1895–1900, watercolour on white paper, Mattioli Collection, Milan, Italy, 30 x 45cm (12 x 18in)

Cézanne's mother's death and the sale of the Jas de Bouffan in 1899 marked a change in his style. As a part-time residence, he rented a place on the estate of the Château Noir. The fragmented light around the building concentrated his attention on specific colours in the landscape. With clear, jewel colours that allowed the white of the paper to create highlights, this watercolour study is almost an abstraction.

Portrait of a Girl, c.1896, oil on canvas, Bucharest National Museum of Art, Romania, 35 x 46cm (13 x 18in)

Cézanne painted at least two portraits of this girl, probably one of the Jas de Bouffan workers' children. As in the painting on the previous page, this has been painted in subdued tones, the bright Impressionist palette has been put to one side, and her face, rather than the impassive mask-like looks of his earlier portraits, shows a rather sad expression.

*Seated Man, c.1898–1900,
oil on canvas,
Nasjonalgalleriet,
Oslo, Norway,
103 x 76cm (41 x 30in)*

This man is neither a peasant nor a gardener, which is unusual for Cézanne's portraits of this period. The identity of the man has not been verified, but Cézanne emphasized his simple dignity with a solid composition and balanced brush marks and colour across the canvas. The entire painting seems to express the hard life of the rural worker.

*Village behind the Trees,
c.1898, oil on canvas,
Kunsthalle, Bremen,
Germany,
65 x 81cm (25 x 31in)*

During the summer of 1898, Cézanne painted in Montgeroult and Marines, both in the vicinity of Paris. While there, he met Denys Cochin, an art lover who bought several of his canvases. This vivid and controlled work has been created with a brush loaded with pigment. The directions of the marks follow the textures of the leafy branches, rooftops and fields. The cubes and triangles of the buildings are distinct within the foliage.

*Mont Sainte-Victoire Seen from Bibémus, c.*1898–1900, oil on canvas, Baltimore Museum of Art, MD, USA, 65 x 81cm (26 x 32in)

In closer proximity to Mont Sainte-Victoire than in his earlier works, Cézanne has treated this familiar view even more than usual as a still life. The main object is the quarry with its dramatic tones and forms. The mountain behind resembles one of his tablecloths. Orange rocks, blue sky, lilac-toned mountain and green trees impart dynamism to the complex arrangement.

Study of Bathers, 1898–1900, oil on canvas, Barnes Foundation, Philadelphia, PA, USA, 73 x 92cm (28 x 36in)

In Ambroise Vollard's biography of Cézanne published in 1914, he wrote, "In the same period as my portrait, Cézanne was also working on some nudes… [he] used drawings he had made previously at the Atelier Suisse and, for the rest, he called upon his memories of the museums…His dream would have been to have nude models pose in the open air, but that was unfeasible for many reasons, the most important being that women, even when clothed, frightened him."

The Large Bathers, 1894–1905, oil on canvas, National Gallery, London, UK, 127 x 196cm (50 x 77in)

Cézanne painted three large-scale female bather groups simultaneously. To concentrate on the overall harmony of the figures, he relinquished naturalism, concentrating on building solid forms, architectural structure and blending brilliant colours. His palette was probably lead white, chrome or cadmium yellow, yellow ochre, Naples yellow, vermilion, red alizarin, red earth, cobalt blue, ultramarine, cerulean blue, emerald green, green earth, viridian and chrome green.

Portrait of Ambroise Vollard, 1899, oil on canvas, Musée du Petit-Palais de la Ville de Paris, Paris, France, 100 x 81cm (39 x 31in)

Throughout October 1899, Vollard posed for Cézanne, frequently being scolded by the artist for moving and making him lose the "line of concentration." Joachim Gasquet recounted: "During many sessions, Cézanne seemed to make only a few brushstrokes but never ceased to devour the sitter with his eyes. The next day, M. Vollard found that the canvas had been advanced by three or four hours of intense work."

Self-portrait with Beret,
1898–1900, oil on canvas,
Museum of Fine Arts,
Boston, MA, USA,
64 x 54cm (25 x 21in)

This is Cézanne's last self-
portrait. It shows a man
who seems to have
resigned himself to
solitude and loneliness,
who has accepted that
by dedicating himself to
his art, he has found the
only comfort possible to
him. Although he looks
remote, he expresssion is
not melancholy, merely
determined, composed and
perhaps a little cross as he
gazes into the distance.

Roofs, c.1898, oil on
canvas, Private Collection,
66 x 82cm (26 x 32in)

Returning to one of the
subjects that had appealed
to him since he first painted
in Pontoise with Pissarro,
Cézanne has focused on the
roofs of houses. The motif
interested him for its
contrasts – in angles, forms
and shapes of organic and
manmade objects. Once
again, this unfinished canvas
serves as a work in progress,
revealing his method of
constructing interlocking
patches of colour to create
form and space.

Bridge across the Pond, 1898, oil on canvas, Pushkin State Museum of Fine Arts, Moscow, Russia, 64 x 79cm (25 x 31in)

Cézanne's preoccupation with expressing the qualities of the landscape was balanced by his concern for the language of painting. Here the oblique, hatched and crosshatched brushwork in many different shades of green, with the elimination of superfluous detail, emphasizes his perception of the constitution of the trees and bridge.

Pyramid of Skulls, c.1898–1900, oil on canvas, Private Collection, 39 x 47cm (15 x 19in)

Skulls had appeared in early work and then disappeared for years. Around 1898, Cézanne painted over ten canvases featuring them again. Much has been written about his thoughts of death and the links with the 'vanitas' tradition (the perils of vanity and certainty of death).

Peonies in a Green Jug, c.1898, oil on canvas, Private Collection, 58 x 66cm (22 x 25in)

Georges Braque originally owned this painting, hanging it in his bedroom, alongside a landscape by his father and one of his own paintings of skulls. He was particularly proud of this picture and always drew attention to it when anyone visited him, explaining that it was an unfinished work straight from the hands of the master. The smoother brushwork shows the diversity of Cézanne's methods.

Inside a Forest, c.1898–9, oil on canvas, Fine Arts Museum, San Francisco, CA, USA, 61 x 81cm (24 x 32in)

In January 1898, Cézanne's old friend Achille Emperaire died. Following the death of his mother the previous October, Cézanne became depressed. In May, Degas bought a Cézanne painting and Vollard exhibited 60 of his works. This unfinished canvas displays all his aspirations of capturing a view through subtleties and contrasts of colour.

Bibémus Quarry, 1898–1900, oil on canvas, Museum Folkwang, Essen, Germany, 65 x 81cm (25 x 31in)

The Bibémus Quarry lies not far from the Château Noir and the village of Le Tholonet. The quarry had been worked by stonecutters in a haphazard way over many years and some of the rock had been cut in precise geometric shapes, while other areas were still in their natural state. Cézanne depicted the various indentations, nooks and crags with broken, layered brushwork that follows the shapes and forms precisely.

Portrait of the Artist Alfred Hauge, 1899, oil on canvas, Norton Gallery and School of Art, West Palm Beach, FL, USA, 72 x 61cm (28 x 24in)

In a fit of anger, Cézanne took a knife to this canvas. He was never happy with it, although he had worked it up to a fairly finished state. It is not one of his finest works. Although he was as comfortable with muted colours as with bright ones, these seem dull and discordant and, as was the case with most of his portraits, the sitter lacks emotion and engagement with viewers.

Bibémus Quarry, 1898, oil on canvas, Barnes Foundation, Philadelphia, PA, USA, 92 x 73cm (36 x 29in)

The emphatic and firm rhythms of Cézanne's parallel brushstrokes create a crisp and complex architecture of interwoven marks across the image, building up a vocabulary of art that no one had seen before. Here, every mark draws viewers' eyes into and around the composition, from the deep greens of the shrubbery and trees to the hatched areas of the amber coloured stone of the quarry.

House on the Banks of Water, 1898, pencil and watercolour on white paper, Private Collection, 32 x 48cm (13 x 19in)

Cézanne spent some time in Fontainebleau, Montgeroult and Marines in the summer of 1898. These locations refreshed him and gave him more material to paint. Watercolour seemed to help him to relax.

Peaches and Carafe,
1900, oil on canvas,
Langmatt Foundation,
Baden, Switzerland,
60 x 73cm (23 x 28in)

Using the same tablecloth
as in several other works,
Cézanne painted this
still life with strong colours.
The shapes are less refined
than many of his other
works and the composition
is not as arresting as
usual. The patterned
cloth contrasts with the
objects on top of it, but
Cézanne was not achieving
what he wanted and
abandoned the painting.

*Lady in Blue, c.*1900,
oil on canvas,
State Hermitage Museum,
St Petersburg, Russia,
90 x 74cm (35 x 29in)

More dynamic and animated
than many of his female
portraits, this, unusually,
is not Hortense, as by this
time she no longer sat for
Cézanne. The woman
appears to be rather sad,
yet dignified and, like the
man with crossed arms
(see opposite), dressed in
smart clothes – perhaps
ready for Church. It has
been suggested that she
may be Madame Brémond,
who was Cézanne's
housekeeper and cook, but
this has not been verified.

Man with Crossed Arms,
1899, oil on canvas,
Guggenheim Museum,
New York, NY, USA,
92 x 73cm (36 x 29in)

Cézanne painted two
portraits of this man sitting
with folded arms. The other
is facing directly out from the
canvas, but in the same
palette of colours. The
model is fairly well dressed,
and the layers of his clothing
have been enhanced with
strong tones and contrasting
colours. Aspects of his figure
and face are depicted from
differing viewpoints, as
Cézanne sought to convey
the whole of the person.

Village Church, c.1900,
oil on canvas, Barnes
Foundation, Philadelphia,
PA, USA,
93 x 74cm (36 x 28in)

With thin paint layered and
juxtaposed into numerous
modulated planes, the village
church in Gardanne rises as
if out of a patchwork quilt.
Once again, in viewing this as
a work in progress, it is
possible to gain a greater
understanding of Cézanne's
various methods. He has
started to convey the effect
of recession and volume
with flat and shaped planes,
obvious brush marks and
patterns made from line,
colour and tonal contrast.

The Three Skulls, c.1900,
oil on canvas,
Detroit Institute
of Art, MI, USA,
35 x 61cm (14 x 24in)

This fairly small painting
has been built up with
strong tones and
harmonious colours.
The strong chiaroscuro is
uncharacteristic, but serves to
bring a monumental feel
to the objects. Constructional
brushstrokes and nuances of
subtle colours help to create
the impression of solidity.

The Grounds of Château Noir,
1900–4, oil on canvas,
National Gallery,
London, UK,
91 x 71cm (36 x 28in)

Returning to the subdued
palette that he often used
at this time, Cézanne
concentrated on a secluded
and rocky ridge to the
north-east of the Château
Noir. As with many of his
later landscapes of this
location, the sky is barely
seen through the trees
and darkness pervades
the wooded area. Apart
from the Château Noir
pictures, he rarely depicted
the landscape of Provence
in this gloomy manner.

Still Life with Watermelon, 1900, pencil and watercolour on paper, Fondation Beyeler, Basel, Switzerland, 32 x 48cm (13 x 19in)

A close-up of a few objects recalls Cézanne's earliest, simple still-life groupings. The difference, however, is that he has flooded the paper with brilliantly-hued watercolours, creating a glowing luminosity that resembles the brightness of many of his oil paintings. His freedom of application with watercolour helped to inform his oil paintings of how form and space could be depicted through colour.

Still Life with Apples, Carafe and Sugar Bowl, 1900–2, pencil and watercolour on paper, Österreichische Galerie Belvedere, Vienna, Austria, 48 x 63cm (19 x 24in)

Short, broken brushstrokes can be seen in this work, as Cézanne's application resembles his oil painting methods. As usual in his watercolours, cursive pencil marks denote the approximate contours of the objects, which are overlaid with touches of vibrant watercolour to define the forms. This is intensely painted, featuring yellows, ochres, reds and blues across the composition.

Sitting Peasant, 1900, oil on canvas, Private Collection, 73 x 60cm (28 x 23in)

Increasingly, Cézanne asked his models to sit facing him. In this way he could create an almost symmetrical composition, such as was formerly reserved for icons. In this picture, the man's arms, upper torso and head form a diamond shape, which is echoed in the wallpaper behind him. The man seems weary and thoughtful, but he remains dignified.

Undergrowth in Provence, 1900–2, oil on canvas, Fondation Beyeler, Basel, Switzerland, 80 x 65cm (31 x 25in)

With little build-up of paint, Cézanne has still created a rich surface of intricate brushwork. This oil painting shares many of his late watercolour characteristics in its brilliance of colour and almost transparent quality. It is not clear exactly where this was or why he did not finish the work, but in its unfinished state, it remains fresh and energetic.

Mont Sainte-Victoire, 1900–2, pencil, gouache and watercolour on paper, Musée d'Orsay, Paris, France, 31 x 48cm (12 x 19in)

Working in the new studio at Les Lauves that he had built since the death of his mother and the loss of the Jas de Bouffan, Cézanne produced numerous paintings of Mont Sainte-Victoire. This watercolour is one of many that he painted directly from his studio window. In cool blues, lavenders, muted pinks and ochres, he has produced a detached and graceful image.

Apples on a Dresser,
c.1900–6, pencil and
watercolour on paper,
Private Collection,
48 x 62cm (18 x 24in)

At the turn of the 20th
century, Cézanne produced
a small group of still life
watercolours that were fairly
large and extremely bright.

The way in which he
applied the paint was
more fluid than in many of
his earlier watercolours
and with more intensity

of colour. The sweeping
pencil marks that he always
made before and during his
paint application reinforce
the contours.

*The Cathedral in Aix from
the Studio at Les Lauves,*
c.1904–6, pencil and
watercolour on
white paper,
Private Collection
32 x 47cm/13 x 19in

The studio at Les Lauves
afforded Cézanne a
panoramic view of Aix and
gave him plenty of material
to paint without even having
to walk out of the door. In
freely applied watercolour,
Cézanne has captured his
sensation of the scene. For
him, 'sensation' was in both
nature and in the mind, but
it was also portrayed
through the touch of the
paintbrush, which he hoped
was then sensed by viewers.

Rocks and Trees, 1900,
oil on canvas,
Barnes Foundation,
Philadelphia, PA, USA,
80 x 64cm (31 x 25in)

Cézanne's struggle to
achieve harmony and
equilibrium in his paintings
remained paramount.
He would return to his
canvases each day and lay
new colours on top of old
ones, adjusting the colours,
harmonies and sizes of his
brush marks across
the entire work. It took a
great deal of time and
effort. Every time he
applied a colour,
he had to make sure
that it harmonized with
the way he envisaged the
rest of the work.

Morning in Provence, 1900,
oil on canvas, 1900–6,
Albright-Knox Art Gallery,
New York, NY, USA,
81 x 63cm (32 x 25in)

For all his apparent
familiarity with his subjects
by this point in his career,
Cézanne kept on studying
and spending days in front

of whatever he was
portraying. He was never
complacent and continued
to strive for ways to make
his paintings reveal more
than superficial appearances
and to be enduring.
Although he admired
Courbet, he believed that
naturalism in art was no
longer relevant.

Still Life with Sugar Basin and Fruit, c.1900, oil on canvas, Private Collection, 46 x 36cm (18 x 14in)

With tiny, overlapping brushstrokes taking on the shapes of each object, the gleaming colours of this still life create a radiant image. But as always, Cézanne was seeking to produce more than just a colourful painting. With his tilting planes, accentuated shadows and glowing highlights, this late composition seems to resolve all the issues that Cézanne had spent his lifetime investigating and striving to resolve.

Bibémus, c.1894–5, oil on canvas, Guggenheim Museum, New York, NY, USA, 72 x 90cm (28 x 35in)

The abandoned quarry of Bibémus suited Cézanne's explorations of distinctions between spatial construction and optical effects. He painted several views with his hatched application of paint. Like a tapestry, his agitated marks and broken patches of complementary colours create rich patterns.

Bathers, 1899–1900, oil on canvas, Musée d'Orsay, Paris, France, 22 x 34cm (8 x 13in)

In this vigorous and dynamic study, the background has been rendered in mainly vertical brush marks, all lively and fairly even. Paint application is undemonstrative in the figures and light curves delineate their contours. It has been built up with lighter opaque pigment over darker colours.

Forest, 1902–4, oil on canvas, National Gallery of Canada, Ottawa, Canada, 81 x 66cm (32 x 26in)

Although he continued to paint locations he knew well, Cézanne rarely repeated them. Even his views of Mont Sainte-Victoire varied.

This view of a forest close to Aix was a place he knew well and where he often painted, but it is completely different from anything he had painted before. With predominantly flat brushes, he applied his angled paint patches uniformly across the canvas.

Blue Landscape, 1904–06, oil on canvas, The State Hermitage Museum, St Petersburg, Russia, 102 x 83cm/41 x 32in,

In 1904, an entire room was devoted to Cézanne's work at the second Salon d'Automne in Paris. Emile

Bernard visited him in Aix for a month and made him aware of just how much he was admired by younger artists. Bernard accompanied Cézanne to the sites of all his motifs. This work, which was painted later in the year, is an enticing composition, filled with his preferred gem-like colours.

Bend in the Forest Road, c.1902–6, oil on canvas, Private Collection, 81 x 65cm (32 x 26in)

The ochre colour of the woodland path points to a motif near the Bibémus quarry. The colour scheme of the forest extends from light green to dark blue-green, while the brushstrokes are almost all applied vertically, avoiding any attempt to express texture. The work seems to herald abstraction, which many later artists would experiment with during the 20th century.

Mont Sainte-Victoire Seen from Les Lauves, 1902–6, pencil and watercolour on two pieces of white paper that have been glued together, Private Collection, 33 x 72cm (13 x 28in)

Even in this soft watercolour, Cézanne has managed to capture Mont Sainte-Victoire's majesty as it rises over the broad plain.

This new viewpoint came from the crest of Les Lauves, a hill north of Aix and the location of his new studio. This unusual panoramic formula has its roots in the topographical sketches of the 18th-century English landscapists. With minimal lines and details, the rugged forms of the mountain can still be seen in the background.

Flowers, after Delacroix, 1902, oil on canvas, Pushkin State Museum of Fine Arts, Moscow, Russia, 77 x 64cm (30 x 25in)

This is a copy of a watercolour by Delacroix that Vollard gave to Cézanne in 1902. On a dark background, the brightly coloured flowers appear to glow. Cézanne has applied his unique touches of unblended colour using a strongly contrasting palette. He remarked: "Technique grows in contact with nature. It consists in seeking to express what one feels, in organizing sensations into personal aesthetics."

The Garden at Les Lauves, c.1906, oil on canvas, Phillips Collection, Washington, USA, 65 x 81cm/25 x 31 in

The studio at Les Lauves stood in ½ acre (0.2 hectare) of land and Cézanne had terraces created; by looking down he could see the garden and looking up, he could see the vistas of Aix. This view is across the walled terrace and depicts the mountains beyond Aix.

*Bathers, c.*1902–6, oil on canvas, Private Collection, 74 x 93cm (29 x 37in)

This large oil sketch is closely related to another two paintings of the theme, one of which is on page 234. This is the smallest and sketchiest of the three and he produced all of them without models. Cezanne said that his purpose in painting this subject was to convey the real distance between the eye and the object.

*Still Life with a Teapot, c.*1902–6, oil on canvas, National Museum of Wales, Cardiff, UK, 61 x 74cm (24 x 29in)

When Cézanne produced his more complex later still lifes, aspects such as folds of cloth, shadows and shapes between and around the objects were treated in the same way as he treated elements in his landscapes. With its curves and vivid colours, this arrangement appears to fall off the canvas; the perspective has been adjusted in order to emphasize the solidity of the objects.

Mont Sainte-Victoire, 1902–6, oil on canvas, Nelson-Atkins Museum of Art, Kansas City, MO, USA, 65 x 81cm (25 x 32in)

This is one of about 60 paintings of this mountain that Cézanne produced. There is no indication of traditional methods of atmospheric perspective to show gradual recession from the foreground to the background and no details in the foreground to imply a closer viewpoint. Instead, Cézanne built up the foreground, middle-ground and background with equally toned, coloured and sized, adjacently placed patches of paint.

The Gardener Vallier,
1905–6, oil on canvas,
E. G. Bührle Collection,
Zürich, Switzerland,
65 x 54cm (25 x 21in)

Apart from a brief journey
to Paris and Fontainebleau in
1904, Cézanne did not leave
Aix for the last two years
of his life. Vallier became
his last model and
Cézanne painted this with
a lively touch, showing the
old man in his best clothes
and hat, sitting in the
sunshine. The painting is
freer than many of the
works he had been painting
recently because Cézanne
abandoned his directional
brushstrokes.

Seated man, 1905–6,
oil on canvas,
Thyssen-Bornemisza
Museum, Madrid, Spain
65 x 54cm/25 x 21in

Another of the portraits of
his gardener that Cézanne
created during the last years
of his life, this was painted in
the garden that Vallier
tended. He sits in front
of the low wall outside
the studio, the sunlight
dappling through the trees.
Thin strokes of diluted
paint build up the upright
figure in light blue and
the contrasting horizontal
ochre wall.

Portrait of Vallier, 1906, oil
on canvas,
Private Collection,
65 x 54cm (25 x 21in)

"I am so slow in my realisa-
tion that it makes me very
sad," Cézanne wrote about
his last paintings of Vallier.
After collapsing during a
violent thunderstorm, he
was carried back to Les
Lauves where his old
housekeeper, Madame
Brémond rubbed his arms
and legs to restore the
circulation. The next day he
continued working on this
painting of Vallier, but fainted
and died a few days later.

INDEX